WORK YOUR CAREER:

Get What You Want from Your Social Sciences or Humanities PhD

Loleen Berdahl and Jonathan Malloy

UNIVERSITY OF TORONTO PRESS

Toronto Buffalo London

Library and Archives Canada Cataloguing in Publication

Berdahl, Loleen, 1970– author
     Work your career : get what you want from your social sciences or humanities PhD / Loleen Berdahl and Jonathan Malloy.

Includes index.
Issued in print and electronic formats.
ISBN 978-1-4875-9427-5 (hardcover). —ISBN 978-1-4875-9426-8 (softcover). —ISBN 978-1-4875-9428-2 (EPUB). —ISBN 978-1-4875-9429-9 (PDF)

     1. Universities and colleges—Graduate work—Handbooks, manuals, etc. 2. Vocational guidance. 3. Counseling in higher education. 4. Doctoral students—Employment. I. Malloy, Jonathan, 1970-, author II. Title.

LB2343.B46 2018   378.1'9425   C2017-907078-9
                                                          C2017-907079-7

We welcome comments and suggestions regarding any aspect of our publications—please feel free to contact us at news@utphighereducation.com or visit our Internet site at utorontopress.com.

North America
5201 Dufferin Street
North York, Ontario, Canada, M3H 5T8

2250 Military Road
Tonawanda, New York, USA, 14150

ORDERS PHONE: 1–800–565–9523
ORDERS FAX: 1–800–221–9985
ORDERS EMAIL: utpbooks@utpress.utoronto.ca

UK, Ireland, and continental Europe
NBN International
Estover Road, Plymouth, PL6 7PY, UK
ORDERS PHONE: 44 (0) 1752 202301
ORDERS FAX: 44 (0) 1752 202333
ORDERS EMAIL: enquiries@nbninternational.com

This book is printed on paper containing 100% post-consumer fibre.

The University of Toronto Press acknowledges the financial support for its publishing activities of the Government of Canada through the Canada Book Fund.

Printed in Canada

ACKNOWLEDGMENTS

This book exists because our University of Toronto Press editor, Mat Buntin, shared our vision and our enthusiasm for this topic. Mat guided the manuscript through blind reviews and provided important feedback throughout the writing process, and we are grateful for his wise direction.

In the process of writing this book, we had numerous prospective, current, and recently completed PhD students across a number of disciplines review chapters and provide feedback. We also consulted with colleagues across the social sciences and humanities to identify how different disciplines conformed to or varied from the general PhD practices we discuss in this book. Further, the University of Toronto Press engaged seven individuals who served as blind peer reviewers for either the proposal and early chapters, the full manuscript, or both. We thank all of these individuals for their constructive suggestions and feedback.

We thank our respective families, Troy, Katie, and Zoë Berdahl, and Ruth, Alida, and Emma Malloy, for their continual support of our own careers.

Finally, as this book is about mentorship and preparing the next generation of PhD students for their future careers, we wish to acknowledge our own mentors: Roger Gibbins (for Loleen) and Graham White (for Jonathan). These two scholars taught us by example the importance of nurturing new scholars, of seeing opportunities for personal agency, and of exemplifying both professionalism and compassion. They taught us how to work our careers. This book intends to continue their legacies.

CONTENTS

CHAPTER 1

GET WHAT YOU WANT FROM YOUR PHD

It's the first week of your PhD program. You're on your way to being a scholar! You will at last meet Professor A, whose work you've always loved. You now have student peers who are just as into intellectual pursuits as you are. You'll be a teaching assistant for a class and finally have a chance to start strutting your stuff. The list of upcoming seminars and visitors for the fall excites you. Your courses have long reading lists, but it's like a smorgasbord menu—everything looks so interesting. Your biggest dilemma is choosing between all these great ideas and potential supervisors and coming up with a dissertation topic. And that dissertation is going to be a bang-up job, rocketing you into your dream academic position where you can cultivate new, enthusiastic young minds.

Fast forward to Year 6 of your PhD program. You know every inch of the floor your department is on and far too much about the strengths and flaws of both the faculty and your fellow students. You're now a course instructor, for the third time, not for experience but because you need the money. No matter what you're doing, you always have a gnawing feeling that you should be working on your dissertation *right now*, but you secretly hope that something (such as a sinkhole swallowing up the university campus) will force you to abandon it all. You have no publications because you wanted to put all effort into getting the dissertation done … last year. Most of all, you have no idea what the future holds. You still hope for an academic job, but you're also buying lottery tickets because the odds are probably the same. But there's no time to muse. You should be writing …

Or consider this alternative future: You finished your program in Year 5 with a strong, tight dissertation that is now in press with a publisher. Two of the dissertation chapters came out as separate journal articles last year. Not that academic publishing is really your priority, with your new position at a national market research firm, a job you picked up through your network and where you'll be applying the research and project management skills you developed in grad school. You are teaching on the side, because you enjoy it, and are getting invitations from departments to apply to their tenure-track positions. Your future possibilities seem endless. And it's all because of how you managed your time and energy during grad school.

Your graduate school experience can end in a number of ways. *Work Your Career: Get What You Want from Your Social Sciences or Humanities PhD* is all about moving from that promising start to a satisfying finish and avoiding the middle outcome—or, if you're currently in that outcome, how to transition out of it. Your definition of satisfaction might not be working in market research, which is fine. The task of this book is to help you identify and reach whatever your particular definition of career satisfaction is.

Individuals who are either considering or enroled in doctoral programs are typically smart and motivated. However, many are unsure about how to prepare for their future careers and are unaware of the importance of being strategic in their choices from the earliest moment possible. *Work Your Career* provides you with motivation and strategies to guide you as you seek to proactively work your career. Rather than moving through your doctoral program with your eyes solely on the next step, we will push you to maximize your personal agency and strategically position that next step into the larger context of your career trajectory. What those steps and trajectory are is ultimately up to you; this book is oriented toward helping you decide what is best for you.

To achieve this, we structure our guidance around an overarching question for you to continuously ask yourself:

> Given both my future goals and the information currently available to me, what is my best decision right now?

We return to this simple but incredibly powerful question within each chapter. Embedded within the question are a number of critical elements that have the potential to change your thinking, your actions, and ultimately your career trajectory. The question forces you to explicitly consider your future goals, and to be realistic as you do so. It pushes you to gather whatever information is available to you and to go beyond relying on what you presume to be true or what your well-meaning but perhaps not fully informed professors and fellow students are telling you. The question demands you use the information you find to weigh your options as you make your choices. And the question requires you to continually reassess your decisions and to make corrections to your path as new information emerges, as circumstances change, and as your goals evolve.

The question is also highly personal. While we suggest a goal for you later in this chapter, ultimately your future goals are yours and yours alone—not your supervisor's, your mother's, your partner's, and certainly not something set "on high" by academia writ large. This is *your* life, your career, your current and future happiness. The best decision for you might not be the best decision for anyone else; one size does not fit all, despite the messages that many students hear (or think they hear). Making the best decisions for yourself will not necessarily result in the exact outcome you predict; life lacks guarantees, and that certainly applies to the advice we provide. But ideally, by asking yourself this question about both your large and small decisions, and by continually returning to the question to reassess and change course as needed, you can avoid any future feeling of regret with respect to your career choices. You can also develop a sense of confidence that you are capable of making the best decisions for yourself and that you can strategically pursue your own best interests.

Answering this overarching question will require you to consider numerous smaller questions and to gather the necessary information to answer these questions. *Work Your Career* is structured around a series of such questions, ordered sequentially from before one starts a doctoral program to when one is entering the job market. While you may be tempted to skip ahead if you are at a later stage, we hope you will take the time (it is a short book!) to read the book straight through. There can be value in considering whether you might have made different choices; at the very least, it can serve as motivation to start applying the question to your decisions moving forward.

With this core philosophy in place, let's get started.

TABLE 1.1 Worksheet: Considering future goals and available information

GIVEN BOTH MY FUTURE GOALS AND THE INFORMATION CURRENTLY AVAILABLE TO ME, WHAT IS MY BEST DECISION RIGHT NOW?	
QUESTIONS TO GET YOU STARTED:	YOUR GUT REACTION ANSWERS:
Future goals:	
■ What kind of tasks do I want to be doing in my future work life?	
■ What would my ideal work day look like? How do I envision balancing my future work and personal lives?	
■ Where do I want to live? How important is that to me?	
■ How much money do I want to make? How important is that to me?	
■ What kind of difference do I want to make in the world? What do I consider to be meaningful work?	
■ What do I like doing, both day to day and over the course of a year or more? What motivates and energizes me? What does the opposite?	
■ Do I like immediate payoff and rewards? Or am I comfortable with investing for the long term, such as through a PhD, even if exact results are not guaranteed?	
Information currently available:	
■ What types of career skills are valued in the sectors that interest me? Do I feel I can build/acquire these skills?	
■ What are the average PhD completion rates in my field? Time to completion rates?	
■ In what careers do PhDs in my field work? Is a PhD necessary to do this work?	
■ Who are recent PhD graduates in my field that I can identify as possible role models (or cautionary tales)?	
■ What are my resources, personal priorities, and personal commitments at this stage of my life? How might they affect my pursuing a PhD?	

Is this book really for me?

Work Your Career has a number of key audiences. One is individuals who are considering or just entering doctoral study, including current or recent undergraduate and master's students, as well as individuals returning to university. If this is you, we are excited about the potential for this book to help you make strategic and informed decisions from day one.

Individuals who are in the early stages of their doctoral programs also have a tremendous amount to gain from this book. At this stage, you are gaining a sense of your interests and aptitudes and confronting a number of "opportunities" that will either serve as important paths to success or distractions that will add time to your program for little gain. If this is you, we are excited about the potential for *Work Your Career* to help you discern what steps are truly in your best interests and will create concrete, career-advancing evidence of your skills. You are well positioned to ensure that the remaining years of your program drive you toward the goals you seek—and to determine if achieving those goals is best met by completing your program or by moving in other directions.

Work Your Career is not just for new or early PhD students, however. For those of you who are finishing, have already completed, or have discontinued your doctoral program, we will help you position yourself, your work, and your experiences to ensure you maximize your competitiveness on the job market. Further, in reading the book (including the earlier chapters), you may realize additional steps you can take in the short term to build your network and develop evidence of your skills. There is still time—there is always still time—to ensure you are making your best decisions in light of your future goals and the information currently available to you. Today seems like a good day to start.

While we speak directly to PhD students in these chapters, we know that many faculty, and in particular PhD supervisors, graduate program chairs, and department chairs, are deeply committed to advancing the success of their students and understand that such success can take numerous forms. If this is you, we believe you will find our approach useful as you assist, guide, and mentor your students. We admire your interest in helping your students prepare for multiple avenues of success and your compassion for them as they do so. We hope this spirit is strong across the academy.

We are well aware that many students return to academic study after working for a number of years, are international students entering the Canadian university system for the first time, are managing physical or mental health disabilities and challenges, or have a range of work, family, and other responsibilities. For these individuals, regardless of your stage in your doctoral program, we believe that *Work Your Career* will be particularly helpful to you as you seek to navigate and learn (or re-learn) the Canadian postsecondary world and balance many competing demands on your time and energy.

Both of us are Canadians working within the Canadian university system, so this book is grounded in Canadian experiences and norms. However, we strongly believe our advice will resonate in a variety of national contexts. Similarly, we intend to speak widely across disciplines. While we are both political scientists, we believe that our approach is appropriate to people across a range of scholarly traditions, particularly other social sciences and the humanities, but also the natural and applied sciences. Our intention is to help new and emerging scholars reach their career goals, regardless of disciplinary context. While some of the specifics will differ, the broad questions and the central theme of how to work your career transcend national and disciplinary audiences. Read on and see what we mean.

Our experience: Loleen

I consider myself to be an accidental academic. I started my undergraduate studies with all intentions of applying to medical school, only to quickly discover that enjoying high school sciences and enjoying university sciences is not the same thing. (Given that I don't like to touch strangers, something that medical doctors are typically required to do, this early discovery was for the best.) My love of the general scientific method and for research and writing drew me to the social sciences, and the applied side of political science really appealed to me. When I went to pursue a graduate degree, I was interested in academia, but I also harboured fantasies of working in politics, or doing government relations for business, or publishing, or .. just something. The ideas were murky, but I sensed excitement and action "out there." I vividly remember a moment as a graduate student driving through downtown Calgary at lunch hour, observing all of the well-dressed, fast-moving office workers and thinking, "I want to be part of that." After I completed my PhD, I applied for a handful of academic positions, but my heart wasn't in it. I was recently married and had no desire to move around the country on limited-term appointments hoping for something permanent. And there were opportunities outside academia that allowed me to use my research and writing skills. Ten years later, an academic opportunity emerged in my home town, and the potential to move my children close to my parents overrode my reluctance to re-enter academic life. Changing careers was hard for me. I found great meaning in my not-for-profit work, and I am grateful to have had the opportunities that I did.

What should my career goal be?

"Wait," you might be saying. "You just told me that my career goals are mine alone. And now you're going to tell me what my goal should be?" Well, yes, at a very high level we are going to suggest one because it will help to position you well.

The question "Given both my future goals and the information currently available to me, what is my best decision right now?" requires you to begin with your future goals in mind. This ensures they drive your choices about how to direct your time and energy. While many students have a single, narrow goal in mind—specifically, a tenure-track university professor position—we encourage you to adopt a broader goal that takes into account all relevant information. Doctoral study is (or at least should be) a transformative life experience that expands your thinking, your skills, and your network. While many students start programs with an eye on a future academic career, the reality is that many doctoral students in the social sciences and humanities do not complete their programs, many who do complete do not end up in academia, and of those who do end up in academia many work for years in short-term positions prior to obtaining their permanent academic position. This information is hopefully not a surprise to you, and it is information that you should consider when strategically planning your future.

The goal that we propose for you is a successful, rewarding career that uses your talents and the skills you developed throughout your education. This career may take a number of forms. This goal is respectful of the realities of the academic job market and is celebratory of the amazing skills and training that PhDs bring to the workforce. It also focuses on your own personal agency: You cannot control job market conditions, but you can take concrete steps to make yourself an attractive employment prospect to a number of sectors. It is critical that you prepare for multiple career options, rather than assuming or preparing for just one, or worse still, drifting along preparing for nothing. What is exciting is that, by approaching your doctoral program with this broader goal in mind, you can work your career to increase your overall chances of success wherever your career path takes you.

Our experience: Jonathan

As an undergraduate, I never planned to pursue a PhD; I was more interested in law or politics, and after my BA I worked at the Ontario legislature. I turned out to be a lousy political staffer, but I discovered I really liked the study of legislatures and political institutions, which led me to graduate school. By that time I definitely had aspirations to an academic career, but I knew the market was poor, and I kept my options open. And my time at the legislature and ongoing exposure to that world meant I encountered people with PhDs working as legislative committee clerks, researchers, lobbyists, and so on. These jobs looked interesting, and I kept those options open, including taking a short contract working in the Ontario government that could have led to a permanent job. In the end, a tenure-track position that asked for my specific background opened up at just the right time, leading me to where I am today. But I am always glad that I kept my mind and options open.

What does "work your career" mean?

PhD career discussions tend to take a bifurcated approach of "academia" or "other," in which academic jobs get the gold star and everything else is some form of consolation prize. We reject this. We don't see non-academic jobs as a "back up" for individuals to pursue when academic careers fail to materialize, and we don't see the competencies and knowledge that one develops during a PhD program as being tangential to success in these careers. We also don't see the attributes that are valued in non-academic jobs as being irrelevant to academic career success. (In what career is the ability to complete projects, meet timelines, work effectively with others, and communicate clearly to a variety of audiences anything but a benefit? Professors need these competencies as much as any other professional.)

We strive for a more seamless and lifelong approach: How do you "do what interests you" throughout your career, regardless of sector? This obviously requires attention to different contexts and disciplines, but we feel that this seamless approach is not only new but also necessary. We strongly believe that by taking a broader approach you will prepare yourself well for a great career, period; preparing yourself for careers in a broadly defined sense will result in a better career regardless of sector, because the competencies are valuable across multiple domains.

To work your career, you need to start building these competencies immediately. If you are just starting your program, you have ample time to make numerous choices with respect to what you study, how you spend your time, and what experiences you seek. If you are near the end of your program, or even if you are done, you still have time to redirect, refine, and reframe your experiences to position yourself effectively. It is never too early—and never too late—to start asking the question that we posed at the start of this chapter and to start making more strategic choices. The middle chapters of this book are devoted to developing career competencies and—importantly—to finding ways to provide clear, irrefutable evidence to potential future employers that you do, in fact, possess these abilities.

Is there a wave of academic jobs coming?

There was a golden age of academic hiring in the late 1960s, leading to perennial predictions of a new golden (or at least bronze) age tied to the retirements of earlier cohorts. But contemporary academic hiring is tied less to retirements and more to government and university finances and changing priorities. A retirement in the department of, say, English might not result in a new hire in English. It might result in a new hire in biochemistry, or some other unit in the university. Or it might not result in a new hire at all. Don't let anyone tell you otherwise. The fact is that the academic job market has two conditions: crappy and really crappy. Some years are better (crappy) than others (really crappy), but the supply of PhDs will always be well ahead of demand. View predictions of a new golden age with extreme skepticism. And be fully aware that PhDs have other opportunities—exciting opportunities, and more opportunities—in numerous sectors.

What career competencies am I building over the course of my doctoral program?

One often hears about "career competencies." The challenge, especially for social science and humanities PhD students, is that it is not clear what exactly this means, nor how you can articulate this to others. PhDs often know that we "know stuff," and we like to believe that we can "do stuff," but explicitly connecting these dots to career opportunities takes thoughtful reflection. We encourage you to start thinking explicitly about the competencies that you want to be able to legitimately claim by the time you leave your program, and then strategically work to establish evidence that you can draw upon, describe, and if necessary show to others to prove you have these abilities. We'll repeat that last point: Evidence in the form of specific experience and tangible outputs is key. It is one thing to say, "I can write clearly and simplify complex topics for a general audience," but it is another thing to back up this claim with copies of your opinion editorial and your report for a local not-for-profit. In the coming chapters, we will provide suggestions for how you can strategically build evidence for the following career competencies:[1]

---

1 These competencies are inspired by and adapted from the National Association of Colleges and Employers, "Career Readiness Defined," accessed 1 February 2018, http://www.naceweb.org/career-readiness/competencies/career-readiness-defined/.

- *Critical thinking and problem solving:* PhD programs in social sciences and humanities naturally train students to obtain, interpret, and use information to analyze issues and address problems. Some students are able to speak to specific quantitative, qualitative, or textual analysis skills, which is fantastic; quantitative skills and statistical literacy in particular can be important career assets. But even if these particular skills are not part of your training, your program and dissertation work will undoubtedly develop your critical thinking and problem solving abilities. Be conscious of the need to articulate this to potential employers.

- *Written and oral communication:* The ability to communicate complex issues clearly and effectively to diverse audiences is a key career asset. One would presume that all social science and humanities PhD students should be able to claim this competency, but sadly this is not always the case, and PhDs can have a reputation for not speaking or writing like normal people. (We were going to use the word "verbosity" there, but it only would prove the point.) Our advice: Take advantage of the incredible opportunity a PhD program gives you to build your communication skills, and identify appropriate publishing and speaking venues that provide evidence of your communication strengths.

- *Digital technology:* Knowledge economy work requires technological ability to complete tasks and solve problems. As a doctoral student, you may be surprised to learn about the wealth of technology training available to you—often for free!—through your university library, IT office, or other units that is unavailable to non-graduate-student mortals. Completing such training can be a wise investment of time (and might cost you a lot of money once you are no longer a student).

- *Professionalism and work ethic:* Productivity. Time management. Project management. Punctuality. Accountability. PhD programs do not necessarily train students in these areas, and while there are many inspiring role models of professors who squash deadlines like bugs, arrive to meetings at least five minutes early with prepared notes, and dress in a manner befitting the profession, there are also ... other role models among the professorate. Disorganization, absent mindedness, and strange spots on one's shirt may have their charms, but not for you.

Professionalism and a firm work ethic are things you should proactively develop as a doctoral student, and we devote all of chapter 7 to this topic. Your goal, we suggest, should be to develop such a strong reputation for your professionalism and positive work habits that your future references (including your PhD supervisor) rave about these qualities on your behalf. Such reputations can be gold. Cultivate yours.

- *Teamwork and collaboration:* Good news! Those annoying team projects with fellow graduate students may benefit you after all, even if you feel like you did all of the work yourself. In all careers, the ability to play well with others is critical. As you work your program, use your curricular and extracurricular activities to create evidence of your ability to build collaborative relationships, work effectively with others, and manage and respect diverse backgrounds and perspectives. Building this competency, and being able to articulate this competency, should be a priority for you.

- *Leadership:* Your doctoral program may or may not provide you with opportunities to develop and demonstrate your ability to lead others. Through your coursework, program, or teaching or research assistant roles you may be provided with a clear project within which you get to organize others and motivate them to complete specific tasks, identify and prioritize action steps, and delegate and supervise tasks. But, more likely, you will need to strategically create your own space to develop and establish evidence of your leadership abilities, possibly by pursuing activities outside of your formal academic program, including a part-time job or a volunteer position, that align with your interests or passions. What you just see as soccer coaching looks like leadership to us. And, more importantly, it can look like that to future employers if you frame it appropriately.

- *Global and intercultural fluency:* The ability to work respectfully with individuals from a range of backgrounds is of increasing importance to many careers. Many social science and humanities programs include coursework that allows you to increase your global and cultural understandings, and your non-program activities afford actual opportunities to engage with individuals from other backgrounds.

As you move forward in your program, be conscious of your current experience with particular competencies and what you can do to develop further. We suggest you create a portfolio that you update monthly with absolutely everything that is even remotely relevant as evidence of your competencies. Future You will be happy you did so.

TABLE 1.2 Worksheet: Creating your portfolio of career competencies

CAREER COMPETENCY	EXAMPLES OF EVIDENCE	YOUR CURRENT EVIDENCE	OPTIONS TO BUILD MORE EVIDENCE
Critical thinking and problem solving	completed two courses in research methods and statistical analysis; designed and administered online survey for cycling club		
Written and oral communication skills	presented research at conference; authored report for local community group		
Digital technology	use of particular software in dissertation; completed software training programs		
Professionalism and work ethic	completed dissertation; completed teaching assistant and research assistant work; managed logistics for local school fundraiser		
Teamwork and collaboration	completed group projects; worked as a member of a research team		
Leadership	teaching experience; served as a not-for-profit board member		
Global/ intercultural fluency	completion of relevant classes; international experience; volunteer for local intercultural association		

Do I really need this book? Won't my supervisor and program train me to work my career?

Ideally, you wouldn't need our advice. Instead, you would learn all this information firsthand from your kind, wonderfully wise mentors. This may occur for some students, but not always. Advising and mentoring grad students is wildly hit and miss, in part because most academics didn't get much mentoring themselves, in part because some are not really gifted in that whole human interaction thing anyway, and in part because many supervisors are only really good at advising people how to follow careers that look exactly like their own.

Professors can talk about almost anything, often at great length. But despite our profession's notorious ability to wax (semi-)poetic on topics large and small, discussing careers is challenging for many supervisors. A diminishing minority of professors started their careers at a time when tenure-track academic jobs were plentiful. The majority (your authors' cohort included) were taught and mentored by that same diminishing minority; while they entered into a competitive job market, they did so being constantly reassured by their supervisors that there was soon to be a wave of academic hiring … any day now. Given this, it is no surprise that many academics, even the most well intentioned, are unable to provide good career mentoring for PhD students: They received little or none themselves.

So, to return to the original question, yes, you really need to read this book, and no, it is not necessarily true that your supervisor or program will train you to work your career, although most faculty are increasingly sensitive to these issues and aim to be as helpful as possible. To be sure, your first source of advice for all these matters should be your supervisor or other faculty in your program. They can provide you with discipline-specific information that is beyond our scope, so we're happy if their advice trumps ours. But one of the crushing facts of life for grad students is that while their scholarly world revolves around their supervisor, the reverse is not true. Your supervisor can't read your mind, and you may not know the right questions to ask. Furthermore, shared intellectual interests don't always mean compatible personalities, which can create professionally vigorous but personally awkward relationships. Some people really click with their supervisors on all levels, especially for this kind of informal mentoring. Others don't. Regardless of how helpful your supervisor is, our advice will help you make the most out of your situation.

Is it "corporatizing" to talk about employment training in a PhD?

When discussing university programs and careers, a common critique is always raised: Universities are not "supposed to" be about employment training, whether at the undergraduate or graduate level. Approaching university education through an employment lens, it is asserted, advances the "corporatization of the university" and loses the true meaning of higher education, which is to enlighten the student through the pursuit of knowledge for its own sake. While we are generally sympathetic to this vision (which always has a beautiful, ivy-covered campus as the backdrop), we feel it does a terrible disservice to doctoral students. Doctoral study is a long-term investment of time and financial resources, and the opportunity costs are large. Moreover, the PhD has *always* been at least in part about employment training; it is just that the employment training was for a specific type of employment (tenure-track academic positions) that is becoming more and more scarce. Fortunately, programs and institutions are increasingly shifting their training to better match the future career needs of doctoral students. At the same time, it is critical for students themselves to strategically orient their own thinking and activities and to work their career. Counting on programs to do this for you is risky.

Why are most PhD programs so focused on academic careers?

This book is not meant to discourage you from aspiring to an academic career; academia is one of the many rewarding career options available to PhDs, and our advice is framed for success in academia as much as other career outcomes. At the same time, there is value in positioning oneself broadly and in recognizing that in many traditional PhD programs various forces funnel students into an exclusive, narrow focus on academic careers.

PhD programs are taught at universities by people who previously earned PhDs and now have tenure-track jobs, and these programs revolve around the study of scholarly peer-reviewed research written by other people at universities with PhDs and tenure. Most faculty have spent their entire careers in the academic world, and part of their own measure of success is producing a new generation of scholars. Having been immersed in a particular set of professional values, they transmit those values to their academic offspring. The funnelling forces toward academic careers are also seen among students themselves. Many students have not explored the diversity of career options: the academic path is clear, while everything else is elusive and eclectic, especially for students working on theoretical projects with limited empirical or "real-world" dimensions. Some suffer from the "unicorn effect," in that they are aware of the challenges of the academic job market but convinced that they are the exception. And students at later stages in their PhDs can get into the mindset that they cannot stop now; they must succeed, and there is one thing universally recognized as success: a tenure-track job.

The more aware you are of these funnels that (intentionally or not) push you toward preparing exclusively for an academic career, the more you can consciously move your thinking beyond this pervasive culture. We suggested earlier that you establish the goal of a successful, rewarding career that uses your talents and the skills you have developed over your education. This may be a career in academia. It may be that your completed PhD opens fabulous doors for you in other sectors. It may also be that your incomplete PhD training is all you needed to get launched in the direction you wanted; there are many successful people who discontinued their PhD program but still credit it for launching their career. Regardless of what success ultimately means for you, strategically positioning yourself starting today is a good choice.

Why should I listen to you two?

Who are we to provide this advice? To start, we each have experience in both the academic and non-academic worlds. Jonathan Malloy worked outside academia prior to completing his PhD; in doing so, he developed an awareness of the career opportunities for PhDs outside of academia and has been writing on the topic since the late 1990s. Loleen Berdahl moved in the opposite direction: after finishing her PhD, she left academia entirely with no intention of returning, worked in a think tank for a decade, and returned to academia with a high degree of reluctance given her enjoyment of non-academic life.

During our years as senior faculty members and department chairs, we have developed particular insight through interactions with PhD students, aspiring PhD students, and recent PhD graduates on a number of levels. We are also both fascinated by and passionately committed to graduate student mentorship. We do not claim exclusive knowledge; there are others who share our commitment. We do feel that our experiences and positions give us a broad view of doctoral careers, and that we have a perspective that is unique from the many other voices on this issue.

Work Your Career seeks to establish a new mindset toward PhD career development in Canada. To do so, we provide practical advice to set you up for a successful career defined in broad and rewarding terms. This advice, as we noted earlier, all links to a single question: Given both my future goals and the information currently available to me, what is my best decision right now? In prompting you to think regularly about this question, we believe that we are establishing sound practices that will serve you well in your career and your life. As our book is intended to inspire a new way of thinking, rather than to be a comprehensive how-to manual or compendium of data and literature, we have deliberately sought to make *Work Your Career* engaging, accessible, and brief.[2]

We boldly believe that *Work Your Career* will add value to your career and life.

....

2 A good scholar never limits their literature to a single source, and we encourage you to read broadly on this topic. We particularly recommend that you access the following: Susan Basalla and Maggie Debelius, *"So What Are You Going to Do with That?" Finding Careers outside Academia*, 3rd ed. (Chicago, IL: University of Chicago Press, 2015); Karen Kelsky, *The Professor Is In: The Essential Guide to Turning Your PhD into a Job* (New York, NY: Three Rivers Press, 2015); National Center for Faculty Development and Diversity (various resources); and Paul Silvia, *How to Write a Lot: A Practical Guide to Productive Academic Writing* (Washington, DC: American Psychological Association, 2007).

Why are you writing this book?

We completed our own PhDs in 1998 and 2000. (Please skip the temptation to calculate our ages. We are each young at heart.) We convocated at a time when there was little discussion of the many career opportunities for PhDs, and we each experienced considerable angst in entering the post-PhD job market. In the two scenarios presented at the start of this chapter, we each sat somewhere between the two extremes, and in hindsight we can see how a more strategic, thoughtful approach would have made the transition from student to career easier and less stressful.

Thus, in many ways, we are writing this book for the current-day equivalent of our past selves. We want you (former us-es) to enter the workforce invigorated, excited, and confident in your ability to create a successful career. We want you (former us-es) to avoid wasting time and energy on things that won't help your career prospects, and to start devoting time and energy to the things that will benefit you.

So, given both your future goals and the information currently available to you, what is your best decision right now? We think it is to keep reading.

CHAPTER 2

SELECT YOUR PROGRAM CAREFULLY

The children's *Choose Your Own Adventure* book series speaks to the dilemmas inherent in making choices. Given a small amount of information, the reader makes a choice, directing them to another section of the book with another small amount of information and another choice. Sections lead to choices, leading to more sections and more choices. At the end, based on the preceding choices, the reader winds up victorious, or not. Contemplating if and where to do a PhD can feel equally fraught. There are so many options, and among those, presumably, is an option or set of options that is right for you and your needs, and another set that is not so good a fit. And your choices, ultimately, can have significant consequences for your overall life in terms of what you learn, who you meet, how much time and money you invest, and your future career prospects.

Have we caused you a small anxiety attack? Fear not! Selecting your program is a perfect place to start applying our question: Given both my future goals and the information currently available to me, what is my best decision right now? Like the adventure book reader, you must make hard choices, but unlike that reader you have the agency to increase your information before doing so. The trick is to know what information you need and how to assess it to make your best decision right now. So let's get to it.

Should I bother reading this chapter if I am already in a PhD program?

There is inherent risk in reading about decisions that one has already made and cannot undo. While you could read everything we have to say in this chapter and think, "Great! I did everything right," some or all of what we have to say may run entirely contrary to choices you have already made, which presents you with an unhappy dilemma: You can either accept our positions and feel bad about your choices (Terrible Option A) or reject our positions and decide this book is complete bunk (Terrible Option B).

We suggest instead Happy Option C: Use this chapter to identify the strengths of your existing decisions so that you can build on these, and to be aware of their limitations so you can proactively bridge or work around them. Ultimately, choices about grad school are less about truly good or bad decisions. Like most things in life, it's more about making the best set of decisions you can … and then making the best of the decisions you made.

How do I decide if a PhD is right for me?

Give careful thought to why you want a PhD and what you hope to get out of it. As much as we emphasize career planning here and throughout the book, choosing to go to grad school ultimately needs to be first and foremost an intellectual decision—you want to pursue knowledge further. If you don't crave knowledge and its pursuit, you've got a hellish few years ahead (as does your potential supervisor) before you likely drop out. Only that craving for knowledge is going to get you through courses, comprehensive exams ("comps"), and your dissertation.

Beyond a thirst for knowledge, though, you should ideally have a career motivation, and this career motivation should be broad in scope. Many students enter programs with clear or vague aspirations for academic careers, but as we discussed in chapter 1, the long-standing uncertainties of the academic job market mean that it is a good idea to not put all your eggs and hopes in one basket. We encourage you to consider *not* applying until you can envisage a number of possible career outcomes, of which "professor" is only one. We should note a particular word of caution to readers who don't really love research and are considering pursuing a PhD purely with the goal of teaching at the university level: We address this more fully in chapter 9, but all university faculty positions, even many or most teaching-focused jobs, carry expectations for research and scholarly publications; if the fire in your belly for research is even somewhat low at the start of your program, your postsecondary teaching dream has a high probability of being realized only in the form of the "sessional trap" (see chapter 8) of teaching individual courses with low pay and limited job security.

Should you pursue a PhD to obtain specific career skills? We discussed career competencies in chapter 1, and in later chapters we will discuss how you can strategically approach your program (chapter 3) and non-program (chapter 4) activities to build these competencies, and how you can communicate these to potential employers (chapter 8). But an important question to ask yourself is this: How will the skills you develop and deepen during your PhD go beyond what you have already developed in your bachelor's and master's degrees? As we wrote in chapter 1, we suggest that your goal should be a successful, rewarding career that uses your talents and the skills you developed throughout your education; it is possible that you already have the education you need to do what you want to do in life. Ideally, your time in a doctoral program will build skills of complexity, depth, and scale that are distinctly different from those of your earlier degrees. If you cannot see a clear path to do so, the considerable time and financial investment in a PhD program becomes more questionable.

You will notice that we do not mention the word "passion" in the decision to pursue a PhD. This is because it is critical to emphasize the practical here. What are the practical reasons why you want to complete a PhD? Unless you are financially independent or have no interest in building a professional career, you need some answers. While a master's degree is an acceptable way to bide time while you decide what to do with your life, the PhD takes up far too much time and money (and leads to such uncertain career options) for anyone to wander in solely to follow a passion. It needs to be part of a plan for your life. The plan can be fuzzy with lots of possible options—in fact, it should be fuzzy with lots of options. But you should still have one.

A final point is directed at mature students who have been out of school for a while and have perhaps enjoyed some professional success, started a family, acquired a mortgage, dog, snow tires, and so forth and are considering returning to do a PhD. Our message is simple: Good for you for considering something new, but take all our advice to think carefully and double it. It is entirely possible that acquiring a PhD may be exactly what you need to move your career and professional goals ahead. Just look before you leap.

Here are some basic facts to keep in mind as you weigh your decision:

1. You don't need a PhD for almost all non-academic jobs.
2. While you do need a PhD for almost all academic jobs, those jobs are few (and possibly decreasing) in number, and pursuing a PhD solely for the purpose of securing that specific type of job is risky.
3. PhD programs remove you from the workforce for a number of years, and you lose earnings and earnings growth during that period. The available data suggest that you will make those earnings up over time, but not in a huge way. During that time, you will likely be living like a grad student while your friends are buying their first homes.
4. For many people, the doctoral study stage of life overlaps with the prime family building time of life. Frankly, having kids is challenging at the best of times. Studying for comprehensive exams or conducting ethnographic fieldwork is, arguably, not the best of times.
5. PhDs *always* take longer than anticipated. While four years is widely bandied about as the "program length," average completion times in the social sciences and humanities can be six years or more, because dissertations take a long time. Completing in four years is unusual.
6. Being part of a PhD program can be intellectually thrilling. There is a reason that it is a life goal for so many people.
7. In completing a PhD, you will develop a number of competencies that are relevant to and valued across a number of careers. (This book will help you do so more clearly and efficiently.) At the same time, a PhD is *not* the only way to develop these competencies, and it may not be the most efficient way to do so.
8. Having a completed PhD is highly satisfying. True, some family members may occasionally refer to the fact that you "aren't a real doctor," but it is a large accomplishment that you will be proud of.

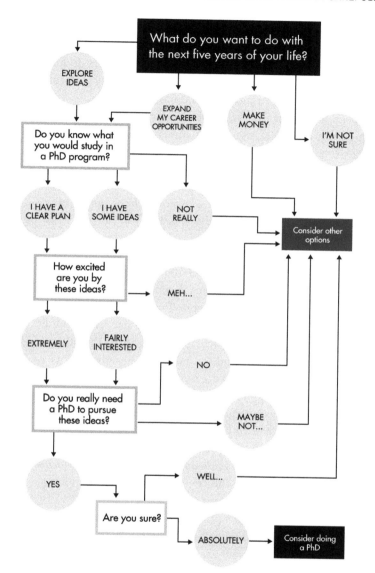

FIGURE 2.1: Should you do a PhD?

In case anything wasn't clear, use our handy decision tree (Figure 2.1) to decide if a PhD is right for you.

Still interested in doing a PhD? Read on.

How do I decide which programs to apply to?

It's remarkable how many aspiring academic researchers do little or flawed research when applying to doctoral programs. Pity your authors here, who in the early 1990s had to do all their program research on paper, looking up addresses and sending snail mail inquiries for brochures. In the online age, the dilemma is working through the cascade of options, so we'll have some pity for you, too. There are so many choices. How do you even decide where to apply (and send your application fee)?

As we said, you need to approach grad school with a plan—a plan that has some options. With that in mind, you can start thinking about initial parameters to consider when sorting through programs.

- *Canadian vs. international:* PhD programs are different in each country, and prospective students do not always realize this until they show up. Coursework is typically more extensive and longer in American PhD programs, where it is standard to admit students directly from the bachelor's program. At the other end of the spectrum, British and Australian PhDs traditionally have no coursework at all, throwing students immediately into the dissertation (although some have introduced coursework and comprehensive exam requirements). Canadian PhDs are in the middle: shorter with less intensive training than American programs, but longer with more preparation than British and Australian ones. And that's just the start of national variations. All of these can be great choices—just keep the basic distinctions in mind as you do your research.
- *Broad vs. specialized program:* Doctoral programs are becoming ever more specialized and niched, meaning somewhere there is a program that probably exactly matches your interests—at least, your *current* interests. It's obviously exciting to think, "This is exactly what I want!" But there are two risks here: (1) your interests can change, and (2) getting too specialized too early means you might not realize your interests have changed, and then wonder why you feel increasingly trapped and miserable. In contrast, a broad, disciplinary-wide program gives you more options and freedom to grow ... grow, or

flounder, that is. Give careful thought to which is best for your career aspirations: A specialized program may lead directly into a related professional field, while a broad program allows more flexibility and a chance to grow and adapt in new directions.

- *Big or small:* Small PhD programs usually mean more faculty attention and a more intimate community, often around shared interests. Large programs have a richer selection of faculty and colleagues. Your fellow PhD program travellers are important here, as they have the potential to be important connections both while you are completing the program and in the decades that follow. Some will be future key professional contacts, working in industry, government, academia, and the not-for-profit sector; some will be future lifelong friends or nemeses. Small programs will naturally have smaller student cohorts (in some cases tiny cohorts), which can mean fewer contacts but the potential for tighter bonds; the reverse is true for larger programs, though you're then not stuck with the same three people for the next 4+ years.

- *Academic vs. professional:* Doctoral programs fall into three (sometimes overlapping) categories: traditional disciplinary PhDs, interdisciplinary programs, and professional doctorates that explicitly or implicitly market themselves as being for people aspiring to non-academic careers. Most universities offer a mix of these with varying degrees of overlap (e.g., professional programs are also likely to bill themselves as interdisciplinary, and faculty may teach and supervise in more than one program). The traditional appeal of the disciplinary programs is that they prepare people in depth for strong academic careers in the core of the discipline; the knock against them is that this is the only thing they tend to do. Interdisciplinary programs are argued to be more innovative; a downside here is that graduates who are interested in academic jobs struggle to position themselves since they don't quite fit in several different disciplines at once and academic hiring committees often want candidates that can teach broad disciplinary courses.

For many, the big question is between the academic and the professional programs, with a fear that choosing one cuts off

TABLE 2.1 Thinking through program options

	PROS	CONS
Canadian	Canada! Possibly close to family.	Canada. Possibly close to family.
International	Opportunity to live in another country and gain international experience. Lifetime ability to casually drop comments like "When I was living in Geneva" into conversations.	Over time, living far from your support network may be isolating, and travelling home can be expensive. You might even grow to miss Aunt Hilda.
Broad	Possible to explore a variety of interests and connect in many directions. A feast of knowledge. So many ways to grow.	Everyone does their own thing in different directions. No one really seems to understand your work. You might feel alone in the crowd.
Specialized	Can address your particular interests, and allows you to spend years with people who are similarly obsessed with a particular niche area.	Your particular interests can change, and the narrow discussions may prove aggravating over time. You may grow to hate the destiny you chose for yourself.
Big	Larger pool of peers and future contacts (networking, right from the start!). Lots of different people and groups.	Sometimes can be a competitive and complex environment where you have to fight for attention.
Small	Potential for a tightly knit cohort and more individual attention from your supervisor and other faculty.	The same small group of people .. for 4+ years ..
Academic	Go deeper and further intellectually than at any other time in your life; clearest pathway to a potential academic career.	If you're not careful and don't keep your options open, this pathway could lead to a difficult career transition period.
Professional	More applied training, with an emphasis on specific skills for a non-academic career. Your program may even make sense to family and friends outside academia.	The risk of a credential that does not carry depth and weight to justify the years invested, with skills that might have been learned elsewhere. A lot of time, money, and work just to get some letters on your business card.

opportunities in the other. The good news is that this is mostly not true: Universities sometimes hire people with professional PhDs, and individuals with academic PhDs flourish in a wide range of sectors. It mostly depends on what you actually do in the PhD—the breadth, depth, and skills you acquire and how you position yourself, which is what this book is all about. If one option strongly resonates with you, go for it. Having said that, traditional academic disciplinary PhDs are the normal default choice.

Having formed a general idea of what sort of programs you are drawn to, you can now sort through which programs to apply to. Here are some things that might influence your decision:

- *Name brand:* Prestigious universities have many strengths—international recognition, deep pools of eminent faculty, fat endowments, and so forth. These can all be good for your grad school and long-term career. On the other hand, prestigious universities can be coasting on their reputations or be such vast operations loaded with egos that there's little time or attention for lowly grad students. They also sometimes offer less funding, since they feel less pressure to compete for students.
- *Bigshot name:* You dream of going to University X to study under the great Professor Y. Nothing wrong with that, and ideally it will be a life-changing experience. But sometimes the dream is rudely crushed. The great scholar may be so busy and overloaded that they barely learn your name, with supervision effectively delegated to a subordinate. And you may discover that the great thinker has an odious personality.
- *Bench strength:* Whether or not there is a Mighty Famous Bigshot, you need to also look at the rest of the faculty in the program. (Be sure to distinguish between different programs on the same campus.) Are there names you recognize or whose research areas look interesting? You want to be sure this is a place where you can feel at home and form a strong supervision committee. Beware again of the above perils of big names, as once you arrive you may well discover a wise mentor who you didn't initially notice. But a good rule of thumb is that

if you don't get excited scrolling through the list of program faculty and their interests, the program is not for you. As we discuss in chapter 3, in social science and humanities disciplines students are often admitted into the program as a whole, then set loose to wander up and down the halls to find a supervisor. (Sort of.) Given this, you want to have a reasonably target-rich environment. This doesn't necessarily mean a long list in your specific subfield, which may indeed just have a couple of people. But they should be backed up by others who can also be of use to you.

- *Program requirements:* While the formats of social science and humanities PhD programs are common enough that we've gone ahead and written this book about them, there can be significant differences even within the same discipline, and even more for interdisciplinary programs. Research these as much as you can, such as what courses are required and how comprehensive exams work. Admittedly, it may be difficult to know what to do with this information, especially if you're just reading it off the program website with no insider knowledge. However, you may come across important or striking things that affect your choices or encourage you to make direct inquiries to the program ("Is it true that every doctoral student has to learn three languages to pass their comps?").

- *Past degrees:* Students are often advised to complete their bachelor's, master's, and PhD degrees at different universities. The reason is that moving between universities exposes students to more faculty, diversifying the students' influences, networks, and opportunities. While this is not possible for everyone, there is general wisdom in this advice, and you should consider looking at options beyond your familiar stomping grounds.

- *Personal:* This is the tricky one. Do you have personal reasons that place geographic restrictions on your choices? The toughest challenge is balancing your interests with those of a partner; you may also have other family obligations or reasons. There's no simple answer here since only you can decide the sacrifices you are willing to make.

There will be tradeoffs among these six considerations for deciding which programs to *apply* to, and we cannot tell you which is most important. But we can say that your decision should not rest overwhelmingly on just one. We are going to say that again—don't make your decision based solely on any one of these. It's fine to have one be the key reason … as long as others are also supporting your decision.

Is doctoral study a good time to have kids?

There is never a "good time" to have kids. As it is sometimes said, if the continuation of the human race depended upon people rationally waiting for the right time to have children, humanity would have died out long ago. As many potential and actual PhD students are of prime childrearing age, two questions will often arise: "Is this the right time to have kids?" and "Is this the right time to do a PhD?" These questions are often of particular concern to female students. While men also struggle with this balancing act, there is considerable evidence that balancing parenthood and academic life at all stages is more challenging for women than for men, with women being more likely to pay a "baby penalty." Challenging this is a structural problem that is beyond the capacity of this book, but it is important to at least understand the reality and how to approach it.

We have no instant answers, but we do suggest that you keep a few things in mind. First, it is hard to truly understand how exhausting babies and young children are until you are living with them full time. They are wonderful, delightful, cute as can be, and they will wake you up in the middle of the night repeatedly for five years or so (or at least it will feel that way). That being said, you will feel this exhaustion whether you are in a doctoral program, working, or a stay-at-home parent. Second, raising children can be more expensive than one anticipates, and managing child care (much less paying for it) can be more complicated than one anticipates. As doctoral programs are not the path to short-term riches, it is important to give careful thought to how potential financial and other stresses will impact your family life. Finally, many aspects of PhD life are more amenable than other lifestyles to young families, particularly the potential for (somewhat) flexible schedules and the ability to work remotely (such as from one's kitchen while the baby naps—oh, please, let the baby nap ..). The challenge lies in making this flexibility work in light of the demands on one's time and energy.

If you are (or plan to be) balancing a PhD program and a young family, your need for strong organizational skills and a clear plan of action, as we recommend throughout this book, is particularly high.

What should I put in my application?

PhD applications typically involve lots of forms and grade transcripts, arranging for reference letters, and writing a plan of study. While the GRE (Graduate Record Examination) is almost universally required by American institutions as a condition of entry, its use is more mixed in Canada and other countries, and many programs do not require it at all. Instead, apart from your grades—which you cannot change—the two substantive areas to focus on are reference letters and the plan of study.

Students in large undergraduate programs often struggle to find good references from faculty who know them more than superficially, though by the time you are applying for a PhD, you will hopefully have some strong relationships with master's professors. The exact importance of letters can vary by program, discipline, and the level of competition; sometimes letters serve mostly as a form of due diligence to ensure the committee is not missing anything, but at other times letters can be the clincher, particularly in highly competitive programs and scholarship decisions. While it is important to get letters that can speak authoritatively about your abilities, it is not the end of the world if you can't find a magical dream mentor to write you the perfect letter. What you can do is ensure your referee has the necessary information to write the best possible reference—supply them with your transcript, résumé/CV, graded assignments from any courses you took from them, and information on why you are applying to a particular program. (We revisit how to get the reference letters you need in chapters 5 and 8).

The plan of study is more crucial, though again not necessarily for the reasons you might expect. While a plan of study is indeed an opportunity to demonstrate your academic depth and potential, it is also an important guide to a committee on whether you will be a good fit and have reasonable prospects for success in a program. Saying you want to study a topic related to Africa in a department that has no Africanists is a bad sign (not to mention an indication of lousy research on your part). This is particularly important for smaller programs that admit just a few students annually.

A difficult challenge is knowing how specific to be. Some plans of study are distressingly vague ("I love studying great thinkers and want to do a dissertation on one of Plato, Aristotle, Machiavelli, Kant, or Nietzsche—they're all so great!"), suggesting that the applicant will indeed love grad school, but will never come up with a plan that allows them to leave it. But other plans are so specific that a committee wonders if there is any potential for growth ("My dissertation will focus on the use of commas in *Anne of Green Gables*") and whether there's any point in the applicant going to grad school at all. A Goldilocks approach is inevitably best—laying out some clear, broad ideas of what you want to look at, but leaving lots of areas to fill in and expand.

Contacting potential supervisors beforehand is generally a good idea; if you think you'd like to work with Professor A, reach out to them by email. They will typically be polite and non-committal, but the resulting correspondence is a chance for both parties to get a superficial but useful idea of each other. If Professor A finds your ideas interesting and thinks they might want to work with you (or doesn't but refers you to Professor B, who does), this will likely boost your application's chances; if not, better to learn that now rather than over the next five years. However, we advise against sending scattershot inquiries to half the department. Do some research and target your inquiries toward specific people, particularly the graduate program supervisor.

In the end, though, grades are typically the biggest single determinant in admissions decisions ... and in the financial offers accompanying admissions decisions.

BOX 2.1: SAMPLE LETTERS TO PROSPECTIVE SUPERVISORS

Bad letter:
Hi. I am thinking of applying for your PhD program and think you might be a good supervisor. [For extra demerit points, write that line separately to several different people in the same department.] I am really interested in [three very different subfields]. I really liked your book [title partially wrong] and would like to work with you. Do you have any research grants and are you looking for research assistants? Can you call me to discuss this?

Joe

Good letter [adapted from a real example]:
Dear Dr. Green,
I am an MA student in [discipline] at the University of X considering applying to the PhD program at [Dr. Green's university]. I am currently working on my thesis under the supervision of Dr. A, due to be completed next summer. My thesis is a study of [blah-blah-blah] entitled ["suitable scholarly title"].

Were I to be accepted to [Dr. Green's university], I would like to continue work on [subfield] under your supervision. I believe that your expertise in [broader field] would provide me with an excellent framework within which to continue my studies of [subfield]. I have attached a tentative research proposal to give you an idea of what shape my dissertation might take.

I look forward to hearing from you.

Sincerely,
Joe McFadden

Should I apply for external funding on my own prior to entering a program?

Absolutely. The most common external funding source in Canada for PhDs is Social Sciences and Humanities Research Council (SSHRC) doctoral fellowships; some provinces also have their own programs. Receiving money is obviously a good thing, but grants can be very competitive, deterring some students from investing the additional time needed to apply for them. Yet, as we explain in chapter 5, the ability to secure money is also a career-relevant skill on its own that you should start developing as soon as possible, making it worthwhile even if you are not successful this time. On top of this, having external funding makes you even more attractive to prospective programs: It shows that you set and achieve goals and gives you a stamp of approval from an external source.

How do I decide which program acceptance to take?

An offer of admission to a doctoral program is normally accompanied by offers of financial assistance. Practices vary here. The offer will generally be a mix of a teaching assistantship (TA) or other paid work and scholarship money. Individual faculty may come up with extra research assistantship (RA) funds as well. Some programs may also offer waivers that cover your graduate tuition—a potentially huge difference to watch for. Some aspects of funding may be one-time and others are guaranteed annually for a specified period (usually four to six years). Some programs may offer specific recruitment incentives, such as a subsidized campus visit to help swing your decision or moving expenses.

Sometimes, though, there is no money offered at all. It is rarely in your interest to pursue a PhD without funding, and practically never in your interest to go into substantial debt, especially right at the beginning of the program, for several reasons. Apart from the basic principle of needing to live and eat while in the program, the uncertainty of what will happen afterward—or even how long the program will take—makes it inadvisable to incur major short-term costs on the assumption of long-term financial gain. This is different from professional degrees in medicine, law, or business, which have moved almost entirely to a model of charging high tuition that drives most students into substantial debt, on the assumption that graduates will reap lucrative career earnings in the end. It's also different than undergraduate programs, where borrowing to earn a university degree is (up to a point) a reasonable investment.

In contrast, a doctoral program is a journey into the unknown, and funding at least provides a partial lifeline through the void. A financial assistance package will rarely cover all your living costs no matter how minimally you live. But it's a start, and a big one. It partly makes up for income you could be earning if you hadn't made the decision to go to grad school. And funding—especially TA or RA work—is professionally validating. It says that someone values your work.

While some professional doctorates may not offer funding packages (under the medical/law school principle above), it is otherwise normal for PhD offers to include money. So what does it mean to receive an "unfunded offer"—that is, admission, but no money? We won't mince words here: Typically, it means you were at the bottom of the admission pool—good enough to be let in, but not valuable enough to pursue aggressively. (This does not necessarily apply if you are an international applicant [i.e., not a Canadian citizen or permanent resident] because funding packages might only be available to Canadian applicants.) An unfunded offer might suggest they see you as a middling prospect and revenue source that will generate tuition and grant dollars for the institution with minimal investment on their part. It's not a good sign. Even if you have the means to get by without funding and without incurring substantial debt (a continuing job, family money, earnings from a previous career, poker winnings, etc.), an unfunded offer suggests the program isn't willing to bet a lot on your success. Having said that, it's still an offer of admission and a chance to prove your worth. But be warned.

More common is to receive offers from a handful of programs, each with different levels of funding. This is much trickier, and if you simply accept the highest figure, you haven't been reading this chapter closely enough. Instead, go back to the earlier points on choosing where to apply, and recall the central theme of not relying on any single factor. That's important here as well.

Let's say you get offers from Universities D and E, and University E's offer is $5,000 above University D's. This is a big enough difference to matter, yet not big enough that it alone should drive your decision. Whether you follow the money depends on what each has to offer. All the earlier points apply—prestige, bench strength, and so on—and possibly new ones such as cost of living and quality of life, since $5,000 makes a difference in those areas. If you have the possibility to visit the departments in question and meet people in person, this can be very helpful, but doing so can be challenging logistically and financially, particularly in a country as large as Canada unless the program provides funding to do so.

As with the applications, only you can truly decide here. Commonly, higher sums come from smaller and/or less prestigious programs that know they need to do more to attract you; bigger, more prestigious programs may offer less, not necessarily because they're stingy but because they have so many more applicants that they don't feel much need to woo you. But there's some good news at this point: You *may* have room to negotiate. When it comes to the initial offer, the figure is usually firm—graduate programs, unlike used car dealers, do not make opening bids expecting you to counteroffer. But if you have two competing offers, the program has an incentive to negotiate and will usually do so, though not in large amounts since most of the funds have already gone out in the initial offers and they usually have to scrounge around to find anything more. But be open with them about who and what they're competing against, and they may well come up with something. In the above example with the $5,000 difference in offers, University D might up its offer by $1,000 or—let's get crazy—$1,500. In contrast, if you have two similar offers, you might squeeze a few extra dollars from one of them, but unless you are a real superstar with a faculty member pushing strongly for your admission, no program is going to get into an expensive bidding war for a prospective graduate student.

Whatever you do, don't take on credit card debt for your program. If you are contemplating a PhD program you are presumably a smart person, and credit card debt is not a wise choice.

Our experience: Jonathan

I applied to four PhD programs and was accepted into two, both of which made similar financial offers. One was at the place where I was currently doing my MA, which was a very good university with a terrific graduate student community. But I chose the other program, at the University of Toronto. Here's why:

- I decided it would be a good idea to go to a third university, increasing my exposure to new ideas and people.
- I liked the U of T's reputation and bench strength, though at the time there was no single faculty member that I particularly wanted to work with.
- I wanted to return to the rich Toronto political and professional environment I had encountered while working at the Ontario legislature, which I felt offered the best variety of long-term career prospects.

What is the difference between a scholarship, teaching assistant (TA), and research assistant (RA) offer?

The funds that programs offer you will have different levels of strings and duties attached. Typically there will be a combination of scholarships and teaching assistantships, or possibly research assistantships as well. Straight scholarship money itself may come with no particular duties or obligations (other than to do well in your program), while teaching or research assistantships are tied to specific work duties.

Teaching assistantships

Teaching assistantships typically involve grading, leading tutorial or laboratory sessions, or some combination of these activities. You will typically be assigned to a specific class for a term, and you will need to ensure that you work your own schedule to accommodate the class schedule. It's essential to recognize that a teaching assistantship is not just convenient money for you—it's a job, and this fact escapes some students. If you ask to vacation to the family cottage at the same time when the final exam grading needs to be completed, chances are good that the course instructor will be highly displeased. When working as a TA, you need to clearly map your responsibilities into your schedule and then work your own coursework and research activities around these teaching responsibilities. The good news is that TAing allows you to develop your skills as a communicator and manager of your time. And developing a reputation as a good TA will enhance your prospects for other work such as research assistantships, opportunities to teach your own courses, and your overall professional standing. Crummy and indifferent TAs are also noticed and remembered, but not in a good way.

Research assistantships

Research assistant funding is typically offered to students by individual faculty members with research grants. Research grant funding frequently stresses graduate student training, so the entire idea behind an RA position is that you will be trained, through the process of doing research, how to do research. What types of tasks can you expect to handle? This will vary by the project, the discipline, the individual faculty member, and—over time—the level of skill and responsibility you demonstrate. In the early stages, the faculty member will likely start you off on broad, lower stakes tasks, such as collecting information for a literature review. Once you have demonstrated competence and trustworthiness, the types of tasks may become more challenging and enriching. You may even be invited to collaborate on research and publishing. However, the supply of research assistantships is not always predictable and requires a good fit between researcher and student. Some turn out to be life-changing opportunities, but others are more perfunctory and strictly transactional. And some are miserable fits that one or both parties eventually regret.

As mentioned, your funding offer will often include a mix of scholarship, TA, and RA funding. In assessing the total package, you should consider the work involved and how you will balance your various responsibilities. You may decide that a smaller offer of straight scholarship funding is more attractive to you than a larger offer that will require a considerable amount of time and attention. On the other hand, TA and RA work allows you to build career-relevant skills, which is an important goal of your doctoral program.

Is there a chance that additional funding opportunities will emerge during the course of my program?

Yes. As you spend time in the program, and as you demonstrate your capabilities, professionalism (see chapter 7), and winning personality, there is a decent chance that faculty members (including, but not necessarily, your supervisor) will approach you to take on additional TA or RA work, and when you are later in your program you may even be given an opportunity to co-teach or teach an undergraduate course.

If these opportunities emerge, you will need to make strategic choices in whether or not accepting these offers is truly in your long-term interests. More money is always nice, and avoiding debt is a key long-term consideration. Additional factors that must be weighed, however, include the risk that you will end up pouring quality time into other people's agendas while rationalizing (sometimes falsely) that it advances your career. Teaching your own course is particularly risky: It may offer double the money of a teaching assistantship, but will be 200–300 per cent more work. In the end, be very careful about accepting anything that does not offer a clear benefit to your future employability. When you consider the costs of another year or two of tuition, living expenses, opportunity costs (i.e., the money you could have been earning if you graduated earlier), plus the increased risk of program incompletion as time drags on, the financial benefits of taking on too much become highly suspect. Consider whether the time devoted to such activities might be better allocated to other activities (such as those outlined in chapter 4) that are truly beneficial to your career.

For these reasons, combined with the fact that additional funding opportunities will not *necessarily* emerge, we feel it is critical that you make your initial decisions based on the assumption that the funding package you accept will be the entirety of your funding for the duration of your program. There is a time in one's life for optimism, but gambling on additional funds emerging for you later in your program is not a great idea.

What do I do if I have already started my program and see things I could have done differently?

Chances are good that there are many great things about the decisions you have made so far. The reasons that motivated your choices undoubtedly had some merit, and it is important to recognize this. There is also the opportunity to use the information you now have to ensure that you make choices moving forward that propel you toward your goals. What are the strengths of your current program, and how can you most fully take advantage of these? Where are the gaps between where you are now and where you want to be leaving your program? The next two chapters will tell you how to take action to fill these gaps.

There is still time. There is always still time.

Our experience: Loleen

I did not have a thought-out approach to my graduate school choices; my decisions were influenced by finances and faculty (see "bench strength," above), but were largely based on personal considerations. The program served me well, despite my somewhat impulsive decision making: I pursued classes in other departments, completed summer statistical training at another university, and did a Fulbright program; furthermore, and importantly, my supervisor and committee members provided me with individual mentorship that shaped my career. While I would engage in more strategic and careful decision making if I were making the decision today, I had a well-rounded experience that has served me well.

So, what should I do?

Part of the fun of *Choose Your Own Adventure* books is seeing how different information and circumstances structure choices and outcomes. There is abundant information available to you as you consider your graduate school options—first the question of whether or not you should really pursue the degree, then what schools to apply to, and finally what offer to accept—but it takes work to obtain this information. As the decisions you make will determine how you spend the next four to six years, it is a wise investment of time and energy.

CHAPTER 3

WORK YOUR PROGRAM

By the time you start a PhD, you've already had close to two decades of education, going back to nice Mr. Clarke in kindergarten, so it all seems pretty familiar. With five or more years of university education completed, it may be tempting to see the PhD as more of the same: You take some classes, read some books, take a test, and write a long paper (or set of papers). But the PhD is fundamentally different from anything you've done before, moving you from *student* to ... *something else*—ideally, a career professional, who is a combination of independent actor, scholar, and general force of nature. The PhD is uniquely open ended and you become more of your own agent over time, with tremendous freedom to manage (or mismanage) your doctoral experience.

Working your program is about making small and large decisions that subtly but importantly help you make this transition from student (with limited agency, following the directions of others) to professional (with agency, making strategic decisions for your long-term goals). We have been encouraging you to be thoughtful and strategic as you make choices, always asking, given both my future goals and the information currently available to me, what is my best decision right now? There are a number of important decisions you will make during your program, and these will be the focus of this chapter. And there is a key (but jarring) question that you need to make at different stages: *Should I continue in my PhD program?* Every PhD student needs to ask this in their own self-interest, but rarely feels permission to do so. We give you that permission. You alone know your best interests, and we encourage you outright to ask it regularly, and to answer it honestly. It's crucial to successfully working your career.

The Seven Stages
OF GRAD SCHOOL

1 I Can't Believe I'm Here. The excitement of the first week. The first seminar with your scholarly idol. Sitting right beside the legendary Professor X at a department talk. Your first gig as a teaching assistant—you get to teach! You have finally found your people. So happy.

2 Imposter. You feel lost in every class and are sure there was a mistake letting you into the program. The comps loom like mountains, as does the stack of ungraded papers in front of you. Your original dissertation idea turned out to not be so original at all. This was a big mistake.

3 The Happy Lifestyle. Coursework and comps are done. Dissertation plan nicely taking shape. TAing has become fun. The faculty mostly know your name. You have good friends in the program and the most personalized study carrel in the department. You've got this.

4 Life is Passing Me By. Usually triggered by meeting an old friend driving a BMW. Your dissertation has hit a serious snag—actually, several—and you don't know what to do. You meet the newest PhDs in Stage One above, and shake your head at their naïveté.

5 The Groove. First scholarly conference paper or publication accepted. You have business cards and can instantly recite your top five transferable skills. The dissertation is rolling, you are teaching your first course, and you are on a first-name basis with all the faculty. Flexing your scholarly muscles feels great.

6 The Abyss. The low point. The dissertation has become an awful thing that just won't die. You avoid your supervisor, and are sure they are avoiding you. You've decided your only true transferable skill is being able to make up and recite transferable skills.

7 Finished. You have concluded your program, either by defending your dissertation or moving on to other opportunities. You are on your way to, or already have arrived at, an exciting position where you can unleash all those skills you built up in that personalized carrel. You are ready for the next stage of your life.

FIGURE 3.1: The seven stages of grad school

How do I select the best courses to advance my future career?

Doctoral coursework has two somewhat contradictory purposes: to broaden you as a scholar on the road to mastery of the discipline, and to support your specific area of interest and dissertation. Ideally, you will leave the coursework stage of your PhD with four things: course credit toward your degree (bare minimum); increased content and disciplinary knowledge; concrete evidence of skill advancement; and a roster of strong referees for your future job searches based on the positive relationship you developed with each course professor.

The amount and type of coursework required can differ considerably across both disciplines and individual programs. Some programs have a common curriculum that all PhDs take with few options; others offer an array of choices, usually organized by disciplinary field; and some, especially interdisciplinary programs, essentially direct you to the graduate course calendar and tell you to design your course plan. The type of courses in a PhD program may include the following:

- *Program-wide courses* (often mandatory): surveys of the discipline; general research methods; dissertation-development courses
- *Field courses*: surveys of a specific subfield
- *Skill courses* (usually tied to your dissertation project): languages, specialized methodologies
- *Elective courses*: a chance to either deepen or broaden your learning

Your course selections, especially in smaller programs, may be fairly limited, but usually you have some choice. How should you make those decisions? Start by considering your coursework as a whole, rather than just a bunch of parts. Think of courses in terms of both *content* and *skill development* and assess your potential courses accordingly. This approach allows you to identify content redundancies (e.g., three courses on Bushwackian theory) and gaps (no courses on Bushwackian history) and skill redundancies (e.g., four courses developing critical thinking and communication competencies) and gaps (no courses developing global fluency). This information allows you to strategically select courses that will allow you to create the knowledge, experiences, and evidence you wish to possess at the end of your program.

To do this type of assessment requires some work on your part before making your decisions. Ask for the course syllabus (or a past version) and ask around. What is the course like? What are the expectations and demands? Look for at least some courses that look different from one another and that ideally do *all of* the following: (1) develop or enhance a clear skill that is (2) applicable in some way to your dissertation and (3) tangible and transferable to your broad career goals. When possible, aim to pick something more applied as opposed to yet another seminar where everyone sits around talking about the weekly stack of readings with two presentations each per term; you are likely to be sufficiently exposed to that format in your mandatory courses.

As you explore options, look into whether you can take courses outside your program. There can be some giant pitfalls here, especially if you have no background (i.e., undergraduate courses) in the other discipline—in which case you may find yourself quickly drowning in their unfamiliar approaches, assumptions, and terminology. But if you see some clear connections with your interests and ambitions (and, ideally, a *skill*), consider branching out.

Even with these assessments complete, you may have options from which to select. Here are some additional factors to consider:

- *Secondary subjects:* There can be value in taking a course in a secondary subfield; you learn new knowledge and it *might* help position you in the academic job market. That being said, don't let it override other criteria; "positioning" is an extraordinarily imprecise game, so don't let it alone drive you into courses that do not excite you or do not clearly provide a tangible payoff.
- *Cross-cutting subjects:* You may be really interested in Topic X, but while various courses touch on X, there is no course specifically on it. You can only select one or two courses, and the choice feels arbitrary. This dilemma is not uncommon, especially if your interests clearly straddle different fields or subfields without a clear home. In this situation, ask yourself which course will be most energizing, engaging, and likely to build the best skills. And the bigger question to ask is whether the cross-cutting topic is truly your focus or whether there is another way to frame your interests.
- *Instructor:* Should you follow the undergraduate mantra of "take the professor, not the course"? Yes and no. A good teacher typically makes for a good course, though at the graduate level

much depends on the particular student cohort in a small class. Graduate courses do offer great chances to impress and connect directly with faculty and build relationships with them, leading to possible future supervisors or committee members, research work, and handy reference letters and introductions to their networks. However, you will have numerous opportunities outside the classroom to interact with faculty, so signing up for Professor Great's course just to get to know her is not always necessary (especially if you're less than completely enthusiastic about the course content, in which case you may un-impress her).

- *Grades:* Should you take courses that risk a lousy grade that will impact your future? You have surely already spent much time wrestling with this basic existential question of university education. Grades become less important as you advance in your career, but they still matter, particularly for scholarships. Answer the question however you answered it in the past, since that strategy successfully got you to this point.

- *Auditing:* While auditing can be a great way to expose yourself further to new and less-familiar ideas (and faculty), without the discipline of grading you are less likely to develop actual new skills and outputs. And while it may be a pleasant three hours every week sitting in on discussions about a mildly interesting topic, your time is likely better spent elsewhere.

What skills will help me excel in my classes?

Courses ideally offer you opportunities both to work with content and to build skills. If you focus on the skill building and keep up with the material, your chances of excelling are greater than if you just aim to keep pace with the material. This is admittedly hard to keep in mind when you look at a huge required reading list. But as with everything, we urge you to think strategically and beyond the immediate task. Key skills that you should work on developing as you complete your classes include the following:

- *How to read quickly:* This is how great scholars get anything done and why your professor assigns a high volume of readings. Why is this a key skill? Because even if you never pick up another scholarly book after your PhD, almost any professional position requires an ability to absorb knowledge quickly, and after absorbing six books per week for 12 weeks (okay, we hope we're exaggerating here), reading a typical government or corporate report will be child's play. As soon in your program as possible, you need to figure out how to master large volumes of knowledge efficiently. Focus on summaries, headings, and key points, and always be looking for the big picture: impact and influence in the discipline; how things connect or polarize. Come up with a note-taking system that works for you, and use it religiously.

- *Oral communication:* Professional positions inevitably place a premium on effective speaking, making presentations, and facilitating discussion, and there is no greater opportunity than a graduate course to build such skills. Nearly all courses come with one or more opportunities—and yes, they are opportunities, not curses—to do oral presentations, lead discussions, and participate effectively in group discussions. The more introverted you are (and many PhDs, including us, are at least partial introverts), the more you may cringe at this, but this is exactly the kind of focused, hopefully affirmative setting to build these vital skills. This includes both preparing impressive and appropriate presentations (and the bonus of getting accustomed to coping with technological breakdowns), verbally communicating your ideas, and facilitating discussion by guiding 10 opinionated grad students through a seminar.

- *Research:* Individual classes tend not to explicitly teach the methods and tools for gathering, organizing, and synthesizing large amounts of information, and students are expected to pick up this skill through experience and practice. That is certainly one option, but it is inefficient and risks leaving gaps in your knowledge. The good news: Most university libraries have highly developed research training sessions available to students and faculty. These sessions are worth your time, and you should seek these out as early in your program as possible because investments in this area will pay large dividends—including increasing your chances for success in your individual classes.

- *Written communication:* The scholarly world has a deeply deserved reputation for inaccessible writing. Graduate courses can even encourage this as students are forced to read through important but turgid work, leaving students with the erroneous impression that impenetrability is the key to great scholarship. We urge you to go the other way; even in graduate courses, well-written work gets noticed and gets better grades. Constantly seek to improve your writing, because this will benefit your career immeasurably. Good writing itself does not necessarily get you a job, but employers regularly lament that many or most prospective applicants can't write well. There are untold writing resources available to you in bookstores, libraries, and online, and while we encourage you to read some of them, there are a few quick starting points that you should begin to employ immediately:

- Pay attention to the quality of writing whenever you read. Why is one author so much more engaging and effective than another? Look at what they do and see what you can emulate (e.g., short sentences are usually better than long ones). Absorb yourself in good non-academic writing—fiction or nonfiction—and some of it may rub off on you.
- Learn to structure your writing. Outline your work and what you are planning to say, then go back and fill in each part. Give yourself time to write in drafts. Have someone else read your work (and pick this someone else carefully). Always proofread.
- Kill passive voice—for heaven's sake, kill that passive voice whenever possible! Shifting to active voice will increase the clarity of your ideas, and as a bonus your word counts will decrease, allowing more space for your ideas and presentation of supporting evidence. Review your work carefully on this front, and then rewrite everything in active voice unless you are making a conscious choice to keep passive voice for style and variety.

How do I select assignment topics within my classes to advance my future career?

We realize we are coming across as ultra-calculating at this point, and that it may seem like we will soon start telling you not to eat breakfast without linking each item to a career competency. (Not spilling food on yourself = professionalism ...) But we can't say enough about the value of thinking about how each part of your graduate program can help to work your career. This doesn't mean every single move has to be part of a grand strategy, but it's important to be alert and always looking for opportunities that fit into a larger plan. We've already talked about skill building in classes, but this also applies to assignment topics themselves. You are no longer an undergraduate, where what is written for the course stays in the course. Ask yourself: Can topics and assignments be linked to something broader so that they live beyond the last day of class and help you in the future?

The most obvious link is to your future dissertation—some assignments allow you to try out and develop ideas in an initial fashion that you might later use in your dissertation work. But other links may be future publishing goals—a course paper could be the foundation of a scholarly article—or some other way to provide clear evidence of a particular skill set, such as coming up with an original data set. Assignments might also give you skills in preparing for the comprehensive exams, especially overviews of the material, and indeed some grad courses are explicitly designed around this mission. Not all courses will give you opportunities like this, of course, but always be alert for possibilities. And eat whatever you want for breakfast.

How can I protect my mental health throughout my program?

Graduate school's blend of intense work and unstructured solitary routines provides multiple potential points of stress across the coursework, comp, and dissertation stages. Individuals who flew through their undergraduate years may find themselves grappling with unfamiliar feelings of heightened stress and a sense of being truly overwhelmed, and some don't fully recognize they are dealing with such feelings. Extenuating circumstances such as money or family issues may be additional factors. Be highly alert to your own wellness and actively seek activities and networks on or off campus that provide balance and support for your life. You likely have access to counselling centres and services that can help you, even if it's just to check in and get an independent assessment of how you're doing. It is critical that you prioritize your health and well-being.

Should I pick my dissertation topic and supervisor before I am done my coursework?

The PhD process looks very linear: complete classes, complete comprehensive exams, complete dissertation proposal, complete dissertation ... completed. But what this model enjoys in simplicity it lacks in efficiency. The classes will take you one to two years, depending on your program. Add a good half-year or more to study for comps and only then, after two to three years, you start writing your dissertation. If your goal is to maximize the time you spend in graduate school this works well, but we suggest there might be a more expedient way.

While disciplinary and even institutional norms can vary, in the social sciences and humanities individuals are often admitted to PhD programs with a general topic and possible supervisor, but with no obligation to stick to them (assuming no specific promises or funding arrangements were made). Instead, students are free to roam the halls, looking for topics and supervisors that they ultimately feel are best suited for their goals. Unfortunately, this can result in indecision. It is possible—though in our view, highly inadvisable—for PhD students to still be unsure of a dissertation topic or even supervisor in their third or fourth year. It is understandable that, in the press of coursework and comps, making a final decision on the dissertation gets put off. And admittedly we warned earlier against deciding too early and showing up on the first day of the program with a rigid and inflexible plan of exactly what you want to study. But in our view, it is crucial to have at least a general idea by the end of your first year in the program *at the very latest*. It is okay to have lots of detail still to fill in, but you should be able to clearly answer the question "What is your dissertation about?" by then.

Of course, choosing a topic and supervisor should go hand in hand. We do not recommend coming up with a fully formed dissertation plan and only then looking for a supervisor's name to add to the front page. Neither do we suggest deciding on Professor Brilliant without really having any idea what you want to do under his guidance. (Professor Brilliant doesn't recommend it either.) Ultimately, while you have tremendous discretion in your dissertation topic, your choice of supervisor is (normally) limited to whoever is available in the program. Keep that in mind.

What should my
DISSERTATION BE ABOUT?

BAD IDEA

✗ Exactly what my supervisor tells me to do.

✗ What several faculty warn me not to do.

✗ Whatever I decide, and then I'll knock on doors until I find a supervisor to attach to it.

✗ An amazing topic that will singlehandedly transform the universe of knowledge as we know it.

✗ The smallest and easiest thing that I think will get approved.

✗ Whatever looks hot.

✗ Whatever will be hot in five years.

Possibly a
GOOD IDEA

✓ Something that I get excited about.

✓ Something that one or more potential supervisors gets excited about.

✓ Something that has both reasonably clear theoretical and empirical aspects to it.

✓ Something that feels challenging but not scary.

✓ Something that I can clearly explain to others.

FIGURE 3.2: What should my dissertation be about?

How do I select a dissertation topic?

All the large themes of this book come into play when developing a dissertation topic. Passion can be good, but not at the expense of practicality. It must be something that energizes you for the long run. It has to clearly be your choice, though with careful listening to others. It has to be firm but not inflexible. Above all else, it should be part of a larger *general* plan that has plenty of flexibility itself but takes you in the direction you want to go. While much of your deliberation will be discipline and field specific, we can offer a few guidelines here.

A first but often overlooked step is to look at some recent finished dissertations—both in your specific field and perhaps more generally in your program. This may be daunting as you scroll through hundreds of pages (be it in the single monograph format adopted by many disciplines or the series of publishable papers format adopted by others) or explore examples of creative options such as an artistic work or visual presentation as permitted in some fields. As you consider recent works, look particularly at the overall question and themes, organizational structures, the methodology and scope of research, and so forth. These will likely vary, possibly to the point that you feel confused about what yours should look like. But looking at a few should give you some definite ideas of the parameters and expectations that should guide your unique project. And don't feel daunted—these people finished their dissertations, didn't they? So can you! (If you want. As we will say repeatedly in this chapter, there is no shame in stopping at any stage here.)

After you have done this, spend some time thinking about what energizes you. You need to balance topics that are of interest to potential future employers but also to you personally. There is an understandable tendency among PhD students to try to be strategic about their dissertation topic, by either choosing a subject that feels hot and in demand or steering away from what looks like an overcrowded area. We urge you not to overthink this, and particularly to avoid thinking that you can "time" the academic job market and pick an area that will be in demand when you finish. Trying to pick a field, much less a dissertation topic, with any real precision this way ("I predict that specialists on the Galápagos Islands are going to be in heavy demand in the next three to seven years") is a very bad idea. Any truly consequential trends will be long term, with some areas in gradual decline and others rising, and there will always be some "staple" areas and skills that are in perpetual demand in both academic and non-academic organizations. Rather than trying to chase a hot area, play to your strengths and do what really interests you and where you can do your best work. Forecasting hiring markets, research grant parameters, and publishing trends with individual-level precision is almost impossible. What can be known, however, is that the dissertation requires a long, sustained period of attention to a topic, and therefore you must be interested in it.

We suggest that the ideal dissertation should *modestly* excite you—enough to keep you going, but not so much that you lose perspective ("This is going to change the world!"). It should feel challenging and like a stretch (if you are going to write about something you already know everything about, why are you in grad school?) but not scary. And it should be of at least modest interest to other people; if you cannot convincingly answer the "so what?" question, there is a problem.

Our experience: Jonathan

When I entered my PhD program in political science, I planned to write a dissertation on a recent government that I found very interesting. But over my first year, I heard several paper presentations and lots of talks that made me think everyone was doing studies on that exact topic, so I soon abandoned the idea. But almost none of that work ever emerged in print, and to date there has yet to be a scholarly publication anything close to what I had planned to do.

Okay, so let's turn to figuring out your topic. Most dissertations in the social sciences and humanities are sparked by either a theoretical *question* or an empirical *object of study*. Developing the topic, then, commonly becomes a question of how to come up with the other. For example, you are fascinated by the *question* of how gender roles are constructed; now you need to come up with some empirical way of exploring this. Or, you are fascinated by youth crime rates as an *object of study*, but you need to come up with a theoretical question to guide your analysis. Stop and think: Are your ideas more about a theoretical question or an empirical phenomena? Have you managed to settle on one and are now trying to figure out the other?

Push yourself to be specific about what interests you. Here's an example: Perhaps you want to study religious fundamentalism in some way relevant to your discipline. But what exactly about fundamentalism are you interested in? Are you looking at it primarily as a set of beliefs, as a social system, its external effects on society, or something else? Are your own views about fundamentalism relevant to the project? Those all affect your *question*. But they also affect your *object of study*: Which religions, and what qualifies as fundamentalism? How important is it to define who and who isn't a fundamentalist? Does your focus include other orthodox groups? Nailing down these empirical parameters reopens theoretical questions about why you are looking at fundamentalism at all. It can become difficult to handle both aspects, and struggling simultaneously with the theoretical and empirical boundaries of a project is not unusual. We urge you to try and nail one of the two down while leaving the other more open, and then gradually try to bring them together as you move forward in your program.

When you are selecting a topic, *practical* considerations are also important and valid—especially family and financial ones. If you have kids, a year of remote fieldwork may simply not be an option. On the other hand, prepare to make sacrifices and stretch as far as you reasonably can. It's okay to build your plan with options and variations that depend on finding additional funding; it's also okay to make decisions on what is affordable and feasible, as long as you can intellectually justify it.

How do I find a supervisor?

The dissertation topic is only half the story; choosing a supervisor (and committee) to guide you is the other. The story ends happiest when both parts are woven together simultaneously.

The relationship between supervisors and students takes many forms, from Great Mentor and Lifelong Friend and Collaborator down to perfunctory but still effective. (We address ineffective relationships below.) Ultimately it is a professional relationship and should be approached that way. You want someone who will guide, prompt, and sometimes push you to excel. Your supervisor also wants something: a student and future peer who will energize them and make them do better in their own work as well.

As with choosing a dissertation topic, a little long-term strategizing can be good, but don't overthink it. A big-name supervisor may open many future doors for you—research assistantships, references, employment opportunities, and so on. But not always. One of the most crushing disappointments of graduate school is finding out that the potential supervisor whose research interests perfectly match yours has a very different personality and working and thinking style than your own. Usually this can be navigated, but it takes time and effort from both sides. Alternatively, a lesser-known individual may be a terrific coach who really guides and stretches you to finish well, while Professor Big Name mainly communicates through garbled emails from airports. Again, there's no firm rule here, though it's quite possible you can build a separate relationship with Professor Big Name (such as having her on your committee) while working with a more attentive supervisor.

Given all of this, a little comparison shopping is fine here. Many, many PhD students end up with a great supervisor who they knew nothing about when they entered the program. (Recall what we said in chapter 2 about bench strength.) Coursework and talking to other grad students should give you an initial sense of individual faculty, and it is a good idea to make appointments with faculty to talk about your interests in brief, no-obligation conversations. Most won't be offended if you keep shopping down the hall—and if they are, they probably wouldn't have been a good supervisor. However, *communicate clearly*. Be open that you are looking for a supervisor and that you are still exploring options. And when you have decided, be sure to ask: "Will you be my dissertation supervisor?" You may get an equivocal answer at first, which is fine. However, some students fail to ask directly, just assuming that of course they will work with Professor Brilliant, while Professor Brilliant vaguely remembers a couple of hallway conversations with a student but can't quite recall their name. Nail this down, or at least ensure it's up to the potential supervisor to give an answer.

The supervisor is typically part of a committee (usually two or three other faculty) for your dissertation. Arrangements vary a lot here, depending on discipline and field, sometimes on university-specific requirements, but perhaps even more on personalities and unit size and culture. Some students work almost exclusively with their supervisor and the committee is not even formed until late in the process; others are more plugged into their entire committee from the start. The involvement of committee members will vary considerably, often based on personality and their level of interest in your work. Sometimes a committee member actually does more than the supervisor, especially if the latter is eminent and busy. Knowing all this is important as you look around. There is an excellent chance that you share close common research interests with Professor A, but actually feel a stronger connection and affinity to Professor B, who is less in your subfield but perhaps shares the same methodological approach as you. Or you might be interested in combining topics X and Y and have to choose between an expert in X or one in Y. Often a well-structured committee can help you straddle these choices. However, be alert for dynamics *among* committee members. It is unlikely that you will inadvertently ask two enemies who have sworn to never be in the same room together to serve on your committee, but you may have people with fundamentally different orientations who will pull you in different directions and can't agree. The best way to avoid this is to ask your supervisor and committee members themselves for suggestions of additional committee members or run possible names by them. Their reactions will tell you what you need to know.

How do I know if I should continue my program after finishing the coursework?

This may seem like a strange question, even though we already warned you at the start that it was coming. Why would you do one to two years of coursework and then discontinue your program? Well, the reality is that for some students a few years of PhD coursework are all that is needed to satisfy their PhD itch. The fit between the program and their interests or personality just isn't there, or a great opportunity has presented itself and continuing the PhD program would be a large opportunity cost. No matter the reason, there is no shame in stopping your PhD program at any stage, including after coursework. Let us say that again, because some people need to hear it multiple times: *There is no shame whatsoever in stopping your PhD program at any stage.*

Is the program energizing you, or draining you? Are you excited to start the next stage, or does it make you feel weary? Does the program seem like something you just need to get through, like a root canal or childbirth, or does it enliven you? You may have mixed answers, since every program will have high and low points and good and bad days. But ask yourself these two key questions: If someone handed you an exit degree in lieu of a PhD, would you happily take it and leave the program? And if you were forced to apply for the next stage of the program, would you make that application? Answer honestly and think about your responses.

These questions are doubly important if you did not receive strong grades in your coursework. The range of acceptable grades for graduate courses is much narrower than undergraduate courses, and failing or receiving a poor grade in any grad course is cause for serious reflection. While a single bad grade can be balanced by good performance in other courses, you need to reflect carefully on what caused it, how important the course is to your overall program, and whether it signifies a broader issue or gap that is likely to affect your future success in the program (e.g., you don't like reading theory; you don't like working with stats in a quantitative-oriented program). More than one bad grade is a real concern, as it truly suggests the program may not be right for you, and you may even be required to withdraw. But regardless, it is essential to think about gaps and problems evident in your course grades and whether or how they can be addressed before investing further time and energy into the PhD.

We are not going to tell anyone to stop their program. We are not going to tell anyone to continue their program, either. But we are going to encourage you to *consciously make the choice about whether or not you continue your program.* You are, as we stated earlier, your own agent and the person who should be acting in your own best interest. Take a pause between the key program stages to make sure that you are *choosing* to go forward, rather than just drifting along.

How much should I fear my comps?

Ah, comps. While they come in different forms, a fundamental stage in most PhD programs is the comprehensive exams (sometimes "qualifying exams," "field exams," etc.) whose purpose is to test your broad knowledge of the discipline or specific fields. Comps act as a filter: They are the most effective method available for PhD programs to identify individuals who have managed to get through their courses but are unlikely to succeed in the program and individuals who are drifting along, not asking themselves the previous question about whether they really should continue in their program. They are deliberately built as big walls—*or at least, they seem big*—that you have to get over.

We are sorry if that sounds scary, so read that last sentence again: *They seem big.* Comps take on legendary status in programs, looming bigger and bigger each week with an impending sense of doom. But it doesn't need to be that way. A comp is just one more stage in the

PhD program, and with good preparation you should be equipped to make it.

Comps typically come in two different models, usually varying by discipline:

- *They decide:* Here, the program identifies a comprehensive reading list, often based on field courses. Your job is to read it and be tested on it, usually on a common exam with a common grading committee. The bad news is that this means you have to read all sorts of things that you find marginal and irrelevant to your dissertation and interests. The good news is that you are likely doing this with others, all working off the same list. This provides great opportunities for study groups and support as you all complain about why you have to read this stuff.
- *You decide:* In this model, you are the primary designer of the comp, with the exam and committee customized for you. You may select from preapproved but smaller subfield lists, or you may construct your own reading list entirely, which is then approved by the program as the basis for your comprehensive exam. The good news is that it's all tailored to your interests, your needs, and your strengths (or at least what you think they are). The bad news is twofold. One is the tendency to overdo things, constructing massive lists of what you think you should know and setting the bar too high for yourself; the second is that you will be studying for your customized comp by yourself, without peer support.

Some comps, especially in the "They Decide" model, are retrospective and based mostly on the field courses you just took; others, normally found under "You Decide," are more prospective and tied to the specific dissertation topic and overseen by the dissertation supervisor. The number of comps you will have to do also varies: Two is typical, but there may be one or three or further subfield exams. They will vary in length of time, question format, and whether there is an oral component in addition to the written part.

Bottom line: Preparation is key here. Use your fear of comps to motivate yourself to be strategic as you prepare.

How do I prepare for my comps?

The best way is to read. The worst way is to ... read. The difference, of course, is how you read, re-read, and process the information. We strongly recommend having a clear plan for comp preparation that goes beyond starting at the top of the reading list and going down.

Remember that a comp is just a big exam, and you've written a lot of exams by this point in your scholarly career. But one reason why PhD students approach comps with such trepidation is that in some cases they haven't written a traditional sit-down exam in years. They feel rusty as they prepare for what feels like the biggest exam of their life. They have to scale up, and they aren't sure how to do that.

To prepare for comps, think again about their purpose: They are about mastering knowledge. They are not meant to turn you into a walking library, able to instantly recall a couple hundred scholarly works in detail. But you should turn into a pretty good library catalogue—knowing what knowledge exists, how it is organized, and where it can be found. Think of yourself as a hawk, soaring above the forest of knowledge and seeing its broad parameters all clearly laid out before you. But with its amazing vision, the hawk can focus on one point and see the details. Similarly, studying for a comp involves both understanding and seeing the whole landscape, and then being able to focus and dive when needed. This is not as challenging as it sounds, provided you have a system, so organize your studying:

1. Rip apart the reading list into categories that make sense.
2. Set up a schedule that is realistic (which might involve some trial and error) but pressures you to keep moving, track progress, and check things off.
3. If you are fortunate enough to have others writing the same exam as you, form a study group. Groups provide a number of benefits, but the most important can be a division of labour, allowing everyone to take an area, read everything in detail, and report back.

Many programs share previous or mock comp exams, especially in the "They Decide" model, so go check immediately. Even if they don't or you are in a "You Decide" model, ask individual faculty for examples and generally for as much information about the format and style of questions as you can get. Past questions may not be a perfect guide to the future, but they come close, and comp study groups typically and wisely spend time talking about how to answer them. Even more importantly, *write answers* to the questions and share them with your comp committee. As with eager undergraduates asking, "Can you look at my paper before I hand it in?" the committee may demur, but you may get some feedback.

More tricky to simulate is the oral component. This has become less common than it used to be, but remains in many programs, either as a mandatory component or as a second chance if the written exam is considered marginal. Again, research the format carefully here, but the most common is a follow-up a few days after the written exam where the examiners ask you to repeat and expand your answers. Ideally, this is a happy do-over where you get to be brilliant twice and have a meaningful intellectual discussion with your committee, but it can be a harrowing experience, especially if your written exam did not go well. Know your examiners, their particular interests and style of questioning, and what their expectations are for good performance in the exam. If you haven't taken courses with them, ask to meet beforehand.

Comps are an ordeal, but slow and steady will usually win the race. Overconfidence and arrogance can be disastrous, but there is no need to lapse into imposter syndrome when you discover you can't know everything about everything. In most cases, a looming comp failure can be seen coming, and the candidate has been told that there are concerns. That doesn't mean a free pass for everyone else, but unless you are instructed otherwise, your program and your examiners believe you are capable of scaling the comp wall. Prove them right.

How do I know if I should continue my program after my comps?

Regardless of the outcome, after your comps you should pause and make a conscious decision about your next steps.

Program rules vary on what happens if you fail a comp; some will allow a second try, or it may mean automatic exit from the program (though be sure to know your rights regarding your ability to appeal a negative outcome). Failing a comp is serious business and is definitely a time to ask yourself again whether you should continue in your program. Recall again that comps are often the only point in a PhD program where the program can truly enforce quality control. Failure is definitely a signal that the program has serious doubts about your ability to succeed in your PhD. It is not a skill test that most people eventually master with a couple of tries and then all is well. Be frank with yourself: What happened? Can you identify clear reasons that can be corrected for next time, such as illness, misreading a key phrase, or temporary blanking on a crucial work? Resist the temptation to blame poor instructions, personal biases, or surprise formats, though admittedly those can be at play. The fact remains that a comp is meant to certify your basic command of the literature and ability to analyze it; it's not an incremental process where practice will eventually make perfect. People do sometimes pass on a second try, but often they do not, for the same reasons as the first time.

But even if you did pass, take a moment. Programs may or may not give you much feedback on your comp performance. Ask for some, and ask people to be frank: Were there concerns? What were your strengths and weaknesses? You may not get much detailed feedback, but pay attention to whatever you do receive (especially if you get individual feedback from each examiner). It may be useful as you move ahead in your program and as you continue to identify and develop your key skills.

So regardless of how well you did in the comps, review again the earlier questions about whether you should continue in your program. Again, there is no shame in stopping your PhD program at any stage. You are, as we stated earlier, your own agent, and you are the person who should be acting in your own best interest.

How do I write a dissertation proposal?

Most programs require some sort of dissertation proposal stage, but the formality and expectations vary enormously. Your program may require a formal defence of the proposal, or it may only suggest it would be nice if you could write a few ideas down at some point. Sometimes it is the focus of a stand-alone thesis-preparation course. Regardless, the proposal will typically lay out your topic, your research question(s), your guiding thesis or argument, your literature review, your methodology and research design, and your planned chapters.

The aphorism "Plans are useless, but planning is indispensable" (usually attributed to World War II general and US President Dwight Eisenhower) applies here. The proposal is important, but not *that* important. It is primarily a way to focus and lay out your ideas and intentions as best you can; it is also an opportunity for your supervisor and committee to formally sign off on them and affirm that they think the project is doable. Yet dissertations may end up with little resemblance to the proposal that launched them for various good reasons. So don't spend a year of your life formulating a proposal document and sweating over every comma. Ideally, the proposal and its various components will come fairly naturally as you develop your ideas. If there is a formal proposal defence, it may feel a bit harsh as it's the one place your committee can really lay out their doubts. However, as with the dissertation defence, everyone wants (or at least should want) you to succeed. The proposal is just a proposal; it is not the dissertation itself. Treat it as a useful exercise to get you thinking clearly about what you will be doing.

How do I work effectively with my supervisor?

Supervisor–student relationships vary considerably and are often a function of personality and individual styles. Your supervisor may be a highly organized person with meticulous routines and schedules who expects you to fit into a monthly meeting slot they have set aside for you. Or you may be the highly organized person while your supervisor is brilliant but elusive and erratic. The onus is on you to adapt to their style. In any career path, "managing up" is a key skill. So figure out how to best manage your supervisor.

We will make one prediction: Your supervisor will emulate the way they were (or feel they were) supervised. There is no Supervisor School for them to learn how to supervise (though some universities may offer some general training and support), and the decentralized, free-range nature of most social science and humanities disciplines means supervisors often have only a vague sense of other models beyond their own experience. It is possible that there will be a close connection between your dissertation and your supervisor's own research agenda; in this scenario, you may also be working as their research assistant, be part of a team with other PhD students or postdocs, or co-publishing with your supervisor. If this is the case, you will likely have a structured relationship with the potential for multiple points of regularized interaction. But the more common norm in humanities and most social sciences is the *peripheral* model: Your supervisor and you may have common interests, but your dissertation topic may have little relation to your supervisor's own agenda and projects, and co-publishing or other collaborations are unusual. The relationship is far less structured ("go away and think; come back when you have something"), allowing for more independence but great perils of neglect; out of sight, out of mind.

In either model, your supervisor is also distracted. You are likely not the only graduate student they are overseeing, and they have their own teaching, research, and service responsibilities. As you are your own agent, you need to take leadership to make sure you stay on the radar and to ensure your supervisor knows your needs, especially in the peripheral model where the natural inclination is to leave you alone. The best and oft-prescribed solution, especially in the initial stages of the dissertation, is to set weekly or monthly meetings that force both of you to check in with each other. However, this schedule is likely to fade over time as you get deeper into the project and have less to update, one of you vanishes for a time on fieldwork or sabbatical, or you move to a different city entirely, so you may need to find new and more creative ways to maintain the relationship. But take initiative to ensure there is a structured pattern of interaction; do not assume your supervisor will do so.

While ideally your supervisor and you will mutually adapt and form a good relationship, unfortunately sometimes things don't go so well. This poses all kinds of challenges, and most crucially the dilemma of discerning when things are beyond repair (see Table 3.1 for thoughts on that front). Our biggest advice is to discreetly talk to others, particularly the graduate or department chair. Do not suffer in silence or feel you have no options in a difficult supervisor relationship. Talking to others will help you gain perspective and understand your options. The supervisory committee can be important here, compensating for the deficiencies of the supervisor—though if you find your whole committee to be against you it may be a sign that your supervisor isn't

TABLE 3.1 Addressing student-supervisor relationship issues

PROBLEM	SUPERVISOR-CAUSED	STUDENT-CAUSED	SOLUTION	BEYOND REPAIR?
Poor communication	Your supervisor is unavailable, physically and/ or intellectually. You get little or no feedback or direction.	You are in touch erratically and unpredictably. You send work to your supervisor "out of nowhere," often with pleas for quick feedback.	- Schedule regular interactions - Establish fixed dates for sending work and reasonable deadlines for responses - Consider looking to your committee for more direction	Usually can be salvaged, especially with a supportive committee. But if patterns recur over and over and your supervisor is out of touch for long periods repeatedly, speak to your grad chair about alternative options.
Contradictory/ ignored advice	Your supervisor tells you different things at different times.	You repeatedly do things your supervisor advised you against or don't do things they advised you to do.	- Document discussions in writing - Follow up on verbal meetings with memos: "As instructed by you, I am doing the following..." - Seek clarity in instructions, even to the point of bluntness	Can sometimes be corrected by better communication of assumptions and expectations. But if your supervisor's vacillations lead to repeated wild-goose chases or junking large chunks of work, it is time for a change.
Personal dislike	You and/or your supervisor increasingly dislike interacting with the other.		- Minimize personal interaction and shift to written communication - Document problems in case of further breakdown/abuse	The relationship can usually continue, though through gritted teeth. A loss of basic civility and professional behaviour indicates a need for change.
Mutual breakdown	Your supervisor and you are on fundamentally different wavelengths and cannot agree on what basic aspects of the dissertation should look like.		- Agree to disagree - Request assistance from the graduate chair to find a solution	While not ideal, agreeing to disagree can work. If you cannot find a new supervisor, that may be a sign that your subject needs to be revised.
Abuse	Your supervisor exploits you personally or intellectually. This may extend to sexual harassment or stealing research and publication credit.		- Know your rights - Create written documentation of any concerns or incidents; if something is bugging you, write it down for later reference/evidence - Do not be afraid to report abuse in confidence to university authorities	If you don't trust your supervisor, ask the grad chair to assign you a new one.

the problem. Be self-reflective, and above all maximize your agency to address the situation as soon as possible.

How can I progress through my dissertation? (Or, "how will I ever get this done?")

Your proposal is done and approved. Now you just have to write the dissertation, right? Well …

No matter how much you have prepared and planned, the dissertation will have twists and turns you never anticipated, numerous potholes, and possibly giant gaps looming in the road ahead. Some of these may seem disastrous, but nearly all can be navigated and overcome. As we said, the dissertation proposal is rarely a perfect roadmap. But it gives you direction and an initial plan.

The twists, turns, and gaps will take many forms. Empirical data turn out to be unavailable or useless. Theoretical approaches lead you into blind alleys. Access to sources is 10 times harder or takes 10 times longer than anticipated. Travel funding falls through. Your language studies suggest you were born to remain unilingual. You find yourself arguing against your initial thesis. And things just generally don't go as you planned. We realize this may sound scary, but our message once again is *this is normal.* Few dissertations proceed absolutely smoothly and most encounter significant challenges. The good news—though perhaps not consoling when, say, the archive you were counting on burns down—is that overcoming these challenges usually makes the dissertation better and *makes you better.* This is the core of the PhD

DISSERTATION PROPOSAL

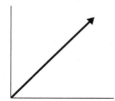

DISSERTATION

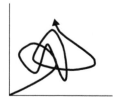

Figure 3.3: Dissertation proposal vs. dissertation (idea adapted from Demetri Martin).

program: not the coursework, not the comps, but pulling off a major intellectual project that no one has done before. An important part of this—and the sign of a mature career professional who is no longer a student—is adapting to circumstances and forging ahead when there is no well-marked trail. You can do it.

Some challenges will be common to almost all PhD candidates, while others will be specific to your project and will often be different by discipline or field. Even the common challenges may require different solutions that suit your circumstances—this is what your supervisor, committee, other faculty, mentors, fellow students, and any other wise people you know are for. Admittedly, it's then an extra challenge to know how to weigh their advice, especially when it conflicts, and sometimes they will have none to offer ("Gosh, that's a toughie. I don't know") or it's even just wrong ("Don't worry about getting turned down by the ethics board; just go ahead anyway"). But this is part of the discernment process as you move from student to career professional; your professors no longer have an answer key or rubric hidden away in their desk. They can give you guidance, but ultimately the creativity and solutions are up to you. And again: You can do it.

Recognize also that *you will never feel you have enough.* There will always be more scholarly literature to read, more cases to examine, more data to gather, more theories and concepts to consider, more examples to give in this list ... While you likely struggled with this already as you formulated your topic and drafted your proposal, it will continue throughout the dissertation. Learning how to set both theoretical and empirical boundaries is important, especially if your initial carefully thought-out parameters aren't working in practice. In most cases, you will be your own worst enemy, while your supervisor and others can cast a more objective eye and let you know that it might be time to stop. On the other hand, if they are pushing you to go further and do more, they are probably right (though see the discussion on discernment in the paragraph above).

Perfectionism can be a huge problem for many dissertations (and scholars at all levels). Sometimes this is about the fear of missing something ("I'd better review my notes for the 124th time"), but other times it's about perpetual improvement ("I just know I can say more here ..."). Avoiding error and improving are both good things, but as with never feeling you have enough, you have to figure out where to draw the line. This doesn't mean settling for mediocre work. But sometimes it means doing what you can, and then going back to revise and improve later.

As you progress with your dissertation, pay careful attention to ensuring your work meets the standards of trust inherent within academia. As a PhD, you presumably know basic rules of academic integrity. But as you move from student to scholar and career professional, the issues and ethical questions may seem greyer. While there is more and more emphasis on disclosing and verifying data, sometimes you may be tempted to do "little" things ("If I just clean up the language in this quotation a little, it will get the point across much better"). Never forget that your reputation depends heavily on being able to see the ethical lines and stay well away from them. Whenever in doubt, seek advice.

It can take a long time to feel you are getting anywhere in your dissertation. It may feel like standing by a pond, throwing pebbles into the water. Each pebble disappears, but if you are throwing them accurately, a pile is building up underwater out of sight that will eventually emerge. Now obviously we think your dissertation is more purposeful and constructive than throwing pebbles in a pond, but the point is to remember that things can still be building even if you can't really see them yet.

How do I know if I should continue my program during the dissertation stage?

Unlike after completing courses and comps, there is no natural moment in the dissertation stage where you can pause and reassess whether you should continue in the program. However, there will certainly be moments—possibly many, many moments—where you will wrestle with this question, especially each year that you re-register and possibly pay hefty new fees. We'll say it again: There is no shame in stopping your PhD program at any stage. You are, we repeat, your own agent and the person who should be acting in your own best interest. At a certain point, it really may be best to stop throwing pebbles in the pond and move on.

But determining this point is very hard. No one avoids significant ups and downs in the dissertation, and there will undoubtedly be times when you can't stand to even *think* about it. (We know of one case—not us—where after the defence the student literally set fire to a copy of her dissertation and danced around the burning embers.) It is hard to distinguish between periods of discouragement and the time to leave.

Mental health challenges are common at all stages of education and in society generally, but can be particularly acute during this stressful period. Depression and other conditions may manifest themselves, and the social isolation of completing a dissertation makes it even more difficult for you and others to understand they are more than the usual ups and downs. We strongly urge you to find supportive people who can help you recognize how you are doing mentally and emotionally and to seek help without hesitation.

Even setting aside depression and other challenges, in any PhD there is a chance of an abyss, a time, usually near the end of the dissertation writing stage, when things seem particularly hopeless. The dissertation may seem to be a dead end that will never be finished, and you may feel alone and disoriented, wondering if you are going in the right direction and whether you will ever finish. Not everyone will experience an abyss, thankfully, but if they do, it is the most likely to shake their confidence that any of this was a good idea and certainly whether they should keep going.

Again, ask the questions we presented earlier. On balance, is your dissertation energizing you, or draining you? Most days, are you excited about it, or does it make you feel weary? Do you at least see some light at the end of the tunnel? Or are you just metaphorically closing your eyes and trying to endure it like a root canal? And if someone handed you an exit degree now, would you happily take it and leave? Some programs after a certain stage do require PhD students to formally apply each year to continue in their program. It is often treated perfunctorily, but we urge you to think very carefully about it. Do you really want to reapply? Or is it time to go? Answer honestly and think about your responses.

Take care of yourself, seek the help of counsellors and trusted others as needed, and give yourself permission to consider all options. Trust your instincts and direction, along with the advice and support of your committee and others. Be confident that you can climb out of the abyss, but also be realistic about whether it is worth the time and effort. In a PhD program, and especially at the dissertation stage, doubts are normal and problems are to be expected. Sometimes it is best to stay, and sometimes it is best to go. Be proud to choose either option.

Our experience: Loleen

I recall my abyss moment (which lasted a few weeks) very well. I was two-thirds completed my dissertation and just did not care about it anymore. A lot of my thinking was reflective of personal factors: I was living in another country with no social support network nearby, and while the university at which I was a visiting scholar provided me with office space, I was choosing to work from my apartment under the assumption that it would be more efficient. (The reality was that it was just socially isolating.) I decided to explore other career options and called a consultant that I found in the yellow pages. (Yes, it was the 1990s.) In that phone call, this kind gentleman asked enough questions—and the right questions—to make me realize I did want to finish my PhD. I have always been grateful to him for speaking to me. And he never charged me a cent.

Can I use a copy editor or a statistical consultant for my work?

A tricky issue for dissertations is whether the student can engage professional help, such as a copy editor or statistical consultant, to "polish" the final product. Practices vary wildly, and your institution and program may or may not provide any automatic guidance here (check your program guidelines/handbook). Some disciplines, programs, and supervisors may find this perfectly acceptable and normal, while others are appalled by the idea. We confess to being closer to the latter—after all, this is a piece of academic work and you are being assessed on it *as its sole author,* so the idea of hiring someone to help with parts of it is concerning. On the other hand, no dissertation is written without specific advice and multiple reviews with marginal notes and corrections from your supervisor and committee, academics regularly review each other's work, and copy editing is a customary stage for academic publications. Thus, it is a bit disingenuous to claim that mature academic work is ever written without at least *some* help.

Certainly any professional help should be fully disclosed to your committee. And what concerns us and most programs is when the assistance goes beyond a passive cleanup of small errors to active rewriting or recalculating. Hiring someone to turn poorly constructed academic work into something passable is not, in our view, acceptable. Seek careful guidance from your supervisor and program on these matters *prior* to seeking out professional assistance; if they are appalled or seem even slightly uncomfortable, you have your answer.

How do I know when my dissertation is done?

We've covered a lot of ground, but an important question remains: What exactly makes a dissertation? And who decides when it is done? This is a difficult question to answer, but one you will likely ask as your supervisor says "just one more draft and that might be it." Your dissertation proposal surely set out some goals and objectives, but determining exactly when they have been met, especially after all the additional twists and turns, can be a challenge.

Even within your discipline or field, there is likely no easy standard for determining when a dissertation is sufficient to go to defence. This is partly because each one is a unique project that is difficult to compare against a set benchmark. But it is also a function of what purpose(s) your particular dissertation is meant to serve in relation to your own future plans and goals.

The escalation of publishing expectations in academia means there is tremendous demand to treat a dissertation as immediately publishable upon completion. But "completed" and "publishable" are not the same thing (except in certain programs that expressly set this standard, especially with the multiple-paper option). Historically, many dissertations were not published at all, or only after years of revision.

But now, many supervisors and committees see their role—really, their duty—as pushing you to not just "complete" the dissertation, but to produce a publishable product that will give you a fighting chance on the academic job market. You need to decide if it's the standard you want to follow. That's not to say the alternative is "no standard." But many dissertations are coherent, original, and well-deserving of a PhD, but are also lumpy, disproportionate, detailed but extremely narrow, or otherwise unlikely to satisfy a publisher or set of journal editors. If you feel that is good enough to suit your future goals, tell your supervisor and committee and ask if they agree.

Supervisors in turn may be somewhat unsure when to declare your quest over, because they are waiting to see how far they can push you. A good supervisor has been coaching you to excel all along, and they want you to be the best you can be. So they may set what seems to be a higher standard for you, because they think you can achieve it. Alternatively—and let's be frank—sometimes dissertations are passed with committees holding their noses. This is when the student has hit some kind of bare minimum and the committee feels they can push the student no further; they made it, though they are unlikely to go further in the academic world. But they're still a doctor of philosophy.

What should I expect for the dissertation defence?

Most PhD programs in Canada have long relied on an oral defence of the dissertation as the final stage of the doctoral program, though there are alternative models such as a written external review that determines whether the dissertation is passable. The lineup varies but typically includes an external examiner from another university, your supervisor and committee, and at least one or two other faculty examiners. In some programs, the defence is a public event—all your fellow PhD students will come watch. In others, it is much more of a closed affair. Some defences are extremely formal (possibly the only time in your program that you're addressed as "Ms." or "Mr." or see your supervisor in a suit) while others are surprisingly relaxed ("Hey, Joe and Linda—which one of you wants to ask the next question?"). You may receive the examiner's report before the defence, or it may be kept top secret. Rules and norms here will vary widely.

To non-academics, the dissertation defence may seem like the toughest stage of all—having to defend your work in front of five, six, or more professors! What a test of fire! But while programs and disciplines will vary, the dissertation defence is generally not meant to be a firing squad where the examiners blast away and see if the candidate survives. In most cases, it is more of a final flourish, but with an immense amount of preparatory work beforehand.

Our biggest tip: *Ask about the procedures*, especially if you haven't had opportunities to watch previous defences. Know what to expect. Take advice on whether and how to make an opening statement, use of technology, and approximately how long it will take (and when and how long you will be asked to leave the room while the committee deliberates). In short, control the stuff you can control.

Ideally, a defence is primarily a conversation about the academic merit and acceptability of your work. Some of the questions may be tough, and it's always wise to prepare for a real grilling since the examiners will feel a duty to be as rigorous as they can be. But—again, *ideally*—the dissertation and you have been well prepared and can withstand their slings and arrows. Your program, and especially your supervisor, should not let you walk into the room unless they are confident you can succeed. And the external examiner should be chosen carefully, as someone who has standing and independent judgment but is not going to be excessively narrow, impossible to please, or arbitrary and petty.

Remember one very important fact in the defence: It is not about the field or topic like a comprehensive exam, but specifically about the dissertation. And who is the expert on your dissertation? *You are*, of course, and you know it far more deeply than anyone else in the room. Prepare well by reviewing it (we guarantee you will occasionally pause and ask, "What was I thinking when I wrote that?") and all the comments from your supervisor and committee. Anticipate lines of questioning and sketch out responses, though there is no need to memorize a script. Your real answers in the defence should be natural and based on your underlying command of the material. Try and think of 10 really tough questions and how you will handle them—and then relax when most of them don't even come up in the defence. In fact, examiners, especially if they are later in the question order, may even feel stuck for questions ("Hey! The external examiner asked all the methodology questions I was planning!") and may use up their time with long comments or speculative questions ("Tell me, how would your study of 1970s disco be different if John F. Kennedy hadn't been assassinated?")

Sometimes things aren't so ideal. The supervisor and program haven't prepared you well. An examiner goes ballistic because you don't mention a particular body of literature. A committee member suddenly decides now is the time to bring up a major concern they've sat on for two years. But while these can be harrowing experiences, the worst-case scenario in such situations is rarely failure but passing with significant revisions—new pages or even an entire chapter (but almost always closer to the former than the latter). This means more work, but unlike all your other dissertation efforts, this one should have clear instructions and a clear finish line. The true worst-case scenario is when the dissertation is not ready but the defence takes place anyway at the insistence of the student against the advice of the supervisor. Typically the relationship between the two has broken down, but sometimes students push the defence because of financial or personal pressures, especially at the end of the academic year. The result may not be pretty, and at best will probably be the nose-holding scenario mentioned above. Don't be that student.

And now you're almost done. You are waiting out in the hall while the committee deliberates (or, quite possibly, is just trying to figure out how to fill in the paperwork). This may take a while and be a painful wait, but eventually they will invite you back in. There is a good chance they may ask for some minor revisions and corrections, and a smaller possibility of major ones as described above. But ... that's it! You did it! You have a PhD! Congratulations!

I am well into my program and didn't do any of this. What can I do now?

There is no perfect student who does every aspect of their program "ideally," and even if one existed, no one would like them very much.

But no matter what stage you are at, you have choices and agency. You can take ownership of where you are now and make whatever adjustments are within your scope of action or influence. And chances are good that you have done at least some of what we describe in this chapter. Start by creating a grid of the career competencies listed in chapter 1. What career competency areas were covered by your coursework? By what you did for your comps? By what you are doing for your dissertation? Where are there gaps? If you can spot areas of truly absent competencies, what resources are available to you as a grad student that you can take advantage of? Above all else, be sure to give yourself credit for the strengths you have developed and the good choices you have made. You made the best decisions you could with the information you had at the time. Now, after reading this book and reflecting more on your experience, you have more information to inform your future decisions. Use it.

So, how can I work my program?

Throughout this chapter, we have returned repeatedly to the idea of personal agency: that you are continually making choices. At each stage, we of course hope that you will return to our guiding question: Given both my future goals and the information currently available to me, what is my best decision right now? While your future goals may remain relatively consistent (and again, we suggested that your future goals should include a successful, rewarding career that uses your talents and the skills you developed over your education), the information currently available will change over time. As you proceed in your program, the knowledge—dare we say wisdom—that you acquire will grow, and your choices will become more nuanced and informed. And at each step, you get to make choices. It is your program, and your life, and no one is going to care about it as much as you do and will. By consciously making the key decisions over your program that align your actions with your goals, you will be doing everything you can to work your program and your career.

Nice Mr. Clarke from kindergarten would be proud of you. And even if he isn't, we are.

CHAPTER 4

GO BEYOND YOUR PROGRAM

A recurring theme in pop culture is to go back and do high school again, usually either with a time machine or a magical reunion weekend. While the idea makes most right-thinking people shudder, it plays off the notion of how past choices shape our present and future, and how inevitably we always wish we could revisit some of our past decisions. It has particular resonance for high school because adolescence is such a confusing, ambiguous, and intense period of life, yet when you look back at it, you can often see things much more clearly and recognize what you would have done differently; rarely is this second sight about the actual schoolwork, but more about the social connections and life opportunities of that unique hothouse period of life (what if your crush liked you back, but you were both too shy to say anything? ...).

We introduce this disturbing idea of lost opportunities because doing a PhD is possibly the next closest experience to high school. Not only does it replicate most of the above features (confusion? check; ambiguity? check; intensity? check; hothouse? check; unrequited love? ... um, hopefully not!), but it is also an experience that many people look back on and think about things they could have done differently beyond the formal program. This chapter is about how to make the most of that experience—the first time. You will be in your doctoral program for years. It can be tempting to think that you should just put your nose to the grindstone (ouch), focus exclusively on your program, and power through to finish as soon as possible. However, this approach has major opportunity costs and—irony of all ironies—may not necessarily get you through your program any more quickly. Your formal doctoral program—the classes, the comps, the dissertation—is the foundation for your career preparation, but it is in your interest to take action to build upon this foundation.

This is a unique period of your life and it is up to you to make the most of it. We continually emphasize personal agency and the need to take ownership for your career as soon as possible. In this vein, you should make it a priority to pursue opportunities beyond your formal academic program and the particular non-program training opportunities available to you as a PhD student. We use the word "priority" very deliberately: We don't just feel you should "try" to squeeze in some activities that are not directly related to your academic program; we argue that you should actually make a strong, concerted effort to do so. Pursuing non-program activities is an investment in your future career, regardless of what sector you end up in. Your return on the investment will be increased information, enhanced skills, and expanded networks—all of which will benefit you in the long run.

Shouldn't I focus solely on my program and dissertation?

Given the long duration of many social science and humanities PhD programs, there is an understandable mantra of "focus on getting the dissertation done." This is sound, in the same way that eating a balanced diet and getting a good night's sleep are important. But just as your life doesn't solely consist of eating and sleeping, getting to and then through the dissertation should not be your only focus. You obviously want to complete your program in a reasonable amount of time to avoid financial and personal strain and to minimize the opportunity costs of being out of the workforce. But opportunity costs cut both ways: If you skip opportunities to build knowledge, skills, networks, and experiences that will help your career, simply to add "PhD" to your name earlier and spend more time unemployed and looking for work, the gain is not entirely clear. You want to use this time of your life as wisely as possible, from the earliest point possible. It can be tempting to ignore the many opportunities outside your program until later (like maybe next term, or perhaps after you have finished a first draft of your dissertation) … after all, you have classes to select, TA work to prepare for, and much more immediate and pressing things on your mind. But by starting immediately—even if you are in your first year—you can make smaller, less concentrated time investments that pay dividends later.

What am I looking to gain from non-program activities?

There are numerous possible benefits from non-program activities, such as doing things that energize you, earning extra money, and just generally being a well-rounded and interesting person. On top of these more personal gains, and assuming that you aim (as we strongly recommend) to position yourself for multiple career options, we suggest you strategically seek to obtain the following:

- *Information:* Making the best decisions requires information, but PhD programs on their own typically leave students surrounded by people working in the same narrow career area and provide little insight into the larger career universe. Increased information, whether obtained through direct experiences, talking to people, workshops, or by other means, gives you an idea of the possibilities and your interests, and opens you up to inspiration—which is always a good thing. It also gives you much-needed strategic insight on what competencies you have and what skills you should develop to enter the job market in a strong position. In most sectors, employers are not looking for PhDs per se, or even individuals trained in particular disciplines. They are looking for career competencies, knowledge, and experience to solve a problem they have (more on that in chapter 8), and many do not realize how PhDs can bring the qualities they are seeking to the job. By planning ahead, you can reduce or eliminate this problem: You will be able to explain how your existing skills and knowledge connect to different environments, and you will identify what additional skills and knowledge you need to build in—and then have the opportunity to develop these.

- *Experience/skill development:* During your program, you obtain and apply numerous skills, but because you are surrounded by others with similar training you may not see these clearly. Further, there are some competencies that benefit your career prospects that are often left underdeveloped over a doctoral program. In chapter 3 we suggested that you assess your formal coursework options through a career competencies lens. Building on this, we encourage you to assess your various activities—your TA or RA work, your volunteer engagements, and so forth—to identify where you already have experience and to identify where you need to be proactive to strategically seek out opportunities. Activities outside your formal program, such as volunteering, internships, and employment, can provide important opportunities to develop both skills and evidence that you have these skills.

- *Networks:* You need other people to advance your career. As a start, you need an inner circle of "close ties," people who will serve as strong references and who are generally invested in your success. But beyond this, you need to develop layers of "weak ties," people who might be willing to make connections for you and alert you to opportunities. It may be that just seeing the word "networking" makes you feel a little queasy and brings up painful memories of the guy who passed out business cards at your uncle's funeral, and in chapter 7 we explain how to network as part of cultivating an overall professional reputation. But here we're highlighting networking and building those "weak ties" as an objective in itself—something that can be achieved, to varying degrees, by effectively working the options below. As with information and skill building, networking and expanding your world of contacts is more effective the earlier you start.

What are the options?

Activities have varying degrees of benefit; some provide information, experience or skill development, and networking opportunities, while others provide just one or two of these, and still others are—how do

TABLE 4.1 Worksheet: Non-program evidence of career competencies

CAREER COMPETENCY	EVIDENCE OF COMPETENCY (EXAMPLES)	YOUR PERSONAL EVIDENCE
Critical thinking and problem solving	Designed and administered online survey of cross-country ski club membership; analyzed results to inform club's official submission to the municipal planning committee	
Written and oral communication skills	Lead author for cross-country ski club's official submission to the municipal planning committee	
Digital technology	Programmed and maintained website for local dog rescue society	
Professionalism	Organized workshop at national conference, including selecting speakers, managing logistics (space, food, audiovisual), event promotion	
Teamwork and collaboration	Worked with three other TAs to develop a common approach to discussion groups and to coordinate grading standards	
Leadership	Served as president of a not-for-profit board for four years	
Global/intercultural fluency	Worked with local refugee settlement group to assist newcomers in their interactions with the school system	

we say this politely?—soul-sucking wastes of time and energy to be avoided at all costs. There are eight basic options for you to consider.

Training programs

Your university undoubtedly offers a cornucopia of short-term training programs, be it through the library, information technology services, or some other unit. On top of this, your faculty of graduate studies or university career centre likely offers their own programs and services, many universities are members of larger consortiums that deliver online services or other programming, and some disciplinary associations offer their own training options. We suggest that you

TABLE 4.2 Activity and likelihood of benefits

	INFORMATION	EXPERIENCE/ SKILLS	NETWORKS
Training Programs	High	Low to high	Low
Experiential Programs	High	High	High
Talks and Events	Low to moderate	None	Moderate
Conferences	Moderate	Low to moderate	High
Teaching and Research Assistant Work	Low to moderate	Moderate to high	Low
Volunteer Activities	Low to moderate	Moderate to high	Moderate to high
Employment	Moderate to high	High	High
Informational Interviews	High	None	High

set a goal of completing one training program of some sort every single term of your program (including the spring/summer term). Start by looking for a general session about preparing for careers. As you move forward, select more tailored classes, such as using citation software or developing methodological expertise, for skills that you can use as you are moving through your program and that you can list on your résumé. As degree completion comes closer, start adding in more applied career classes, such as developing CVs and résumés. If available to you, we strongly recommend sales and business skills courses; these classes help you learn how your competencies are marketable and can add value to employers across the academic, industry, government, and not-for-profit sectors as well as your own self-employment prospects. If your university does not offer a training program that you need, don't be afraid to ask about the possibility of establishing such a course. They may be able to accommodate you or direct you elsewhere.

Experiential programs

Training programs will only take you so far. It is one thing to listen to a speaker, or read a book (even this one), apply a skill in a workshop, or speak to a career coach, and it is quite another to learn through experience. Formal internships, apprenticeships, and other structured work experiences seek to consciously build career competencies and do not presume that the student will necessarily pick up the learning benefits of work engagement passively or implicitly. There is a range of possible activities, with varying time commitments and financial compensation. When you explore the options, don't assume that the suggested disciplinary labels are necessarily indications that the opportunities are limited to those disciplines.

Talks and events

As a PhD student, you will have many great opportunities on your campus that you may never have again; not until PhD candidates leave their programs do they realize that a steady stream of visiting speakers and seminars is not normal in other organizations and workplaces. It can be difficult and even overwhelming to figure out which ones to attend, with many guest speakers, talks, and events calling for your attention. Other types of university events include symposiums, receptions, and other primarily social gatherings that bridge different parts of the university and external communities. The intellectual value of these may vary (as can the quality of the food), but they can be excellent opportunities to expose yourself to different ideas, meet new people, and generally build connections outside your program and disciplinary world.

Many PhD students massively underinvest here, focused as they are on their own work, but it is strategically important to go to things outside your immediate focus. Some activities will contribute to your own intellectual stimulation, which is why universities support them in the first place. Other activities build and reinforce important connections. You may view departmental social events like the holiday reception as tedious distractions from your real work—because they can be—but an hour or two of interacting with other students (who may serve as future contacts), faculty (who may serve as future job references), and the department chair (who is in charge of teaching assignments) can be a good investment.

On the other hand, since there is indeed a strong risk of distraction, develop a strategy for deciding which events are worth your time. For most people, the strategy is simple: Is the topic in your area

TABLE 4.3 Should I attend the event?

Is the time reasonable and not hugely disruptive to my schedule?	Yes: 5 pts No: 0 pts
Is there a chance I will learn something or enjoy at least some of it?	Yes: 20 pts No: 0 pts
How many people will be there?	Less than 20: 10 pts 20–49: 5 pts 50+: 0 pts
Is it primarily a program event (sitting and listening) or an interactive event (e.g., reception)?	Program: 0 pts Interactive: 10 pts
Are there specific people attending that I want to meet?	Yes: 20 pts No: 0 pts
Will my presence or absence be noted, and if so, will anyone care?	Yes and yes: 10 pts Yes and no: 5 pts No: 0 pts
Is it a job talk in or related to my discipline?	Yes: 50 pts No: 0 pts

Scoring:

0–10: Feel free to skip it.

15–30: Debatable use of time.

30+: Go!

This scoring, you will note, has you attending every single job talk that you can, even if you have decided that you do not want an academic career, or even if the topic has nothing to do with your own interests, or even if you have to rearrange things in your schedule to attend. You are not attending for content (although learning new things is always good). You are attending to watch and see what works, and what doesn't work, in presenting oneself for the job market, and how presenters can effectively respond to challenging questions.

of interest? We challenge you to go beyond that, though, looking for things that offer possibilities to push your boundaries and expand your world—for example, learning new methodologies, ideas, and approaches that sound interesting, or connecting with people who can ask challenging questions about your own work.

Our experience: Jonathan

One of the most important aspects of my doctoral education was attending weekly speaker seminars. My department invested heavily in bringing in Canadian and international visitors from across the discipline, and I was a faithful attender every Friday afternoon, no matter what the topic. I sometimes (often?) had almost no idea what people were talking about. But at the end of the talk I always knew a little bit more than I did before, and I gained a much broader and deeper understanding of the discipline, as well as different methodologies, presentation styles, and intellectual outlooks. It was also a chance to see the departmental faculty in action and connect with many of them. Not all programs can afford to invest as heavily here, but this was a fundamental aspect of my PhD program and intellectual development and an incredible immersion into the world of academia.

Conferences

Conferences are part of being a career professional. They are an important way to exchange ideas and build interpersonal connections. They can also be key instruments of professional socialization, with many people of the same ilk gathered in one place and learning and reinforcing certain norms. While conferences are a time and financial investment, there are numerous payoffs. One is new ideas. Listen. Go to panels; some will be duds, but some will surprise you. A good conference experience often involves hearing for the first time about a new theme, book, or thinker, then at a subsequent panel hearing it again, and realizing this is something you should check out. Another is new connections: Meeting people at conferences is a critical way to build your professional reputation and network. And a final payoff is having fun! Dinners and receptions can be more relaxed than you might think, and whether or not you make those professional connections, you can always make some possibly lifelong friends.

As a PhD candidate, you will be automatically encouraged to attend and present at academic conferences. Most academic conferences involve an open call for participants, and the primary activity of the conference is going to each other's presentations. It is also useful to consider professional conferences, which are typically limited to keynote speakers and plenary sessions and are typically more expensive (but with better food). Of potential interest are those oriented around ideas and that solicit newcomers and external participants, rather than the annual gathering of widget manufacturers. Examples here might include conferences devoted to public issues and ideas, which may have a direct connection to your work, and professional development conferences, which may be oriented around a particular profession or themes, like leadership. Regardless of the conference, seek advice from your supervisor or others on whether you are likely to get a good return on your investment.

Academic conferences: Poster or paper?

Academic conferences in the social sciences and humanities tend to have a certain uniformity, not only in Canada but also beyond, with a time-honoured model of a panel of usually three people each presenting their research, followed by a discussant who has read the papers beforehand and prepared comments, and then questions from the audience. The chief alternative is poster presentations, where the research is laid out on a large visual display, the author may be standing by to answer questions, and there may or may not be an actual written paper. Posters can give you more freedom and be more effective at reaching people beyond the tiny audiences at many panels, but they are sometimes viewed warily in the humanities and most social sciences as interlopers from the STEM disciplines (in our view unjustly). Posters are often well thought out, while a time-honoured joke is that papers are written or read on the plane flying to the conference.

The official reason to go to academic conferences is usually to present new research (hopefully a dissertation chapter) and receive feedback on it. But realistically, getting meaningful feedback on a conference paper or poster should be considered a bonus. Assigned discussants are often hit and miss—even diligent ones often struggle with papers and disparate panels that just aren't in their main area of competence—and audiences for papers and posters alike can be small with wildly random questions. Ideally you will receive some great feedback, but the true payoff is the discipline of forcing yourself to write the paper or visualize your work in the first place, and to think about how to summarize it in 15 minutes or a poster.

Which should you pick? Consider both your PhD stage and your existing experiences. If you are at an earlier stage in your program or you have experience presenting a paper, consider going for a poster. Later in your program, aim to get some conference presentation experience under your belt. And regardless of where you are in your program, look into thesis summary competitions. Being able to present your work in two or three minutes is a crucial skill that you will never regret developing.

Teaching and research assistant work

TA and RA work should serve two functions. One, as discussed in chapter 2, is financial support to get you through your PhD, which is a pretty good reason. But the second is to build your professional competencies, and there is always a risk that focusing too much on the first makes you lose sight of the second. Just as you can make a compelling argument that your completed dissertation is evidence of project management abilities (it demonstrates that you can set long-term goals, break them down into smaller components, and achieve them, and that you can strategize different approaches and make effective decisions about the path forward), your TA and RA work are important opportunities for competency development. The challenge is to see it as such, to seek out the right opportunities that give you the best investment of your time, and to carefully document the tasks and translate these into associated career competencies. For TAing, opportunities to interact directly with students rather than just marking a big stack of papers are almost always more desirable; while leading a bored discussion group at 8:30 a.m. Monday may not be an energizing experience, it builds competencies such as oral communication, leadership, perhaps intercultural fluency, and others.

RA work varies immensely but—good news—grant agencies tend to require RA work to be tied to building specific skills and competencies, not just hours of data entry. And if you do end up entering data, that's okay up to a point; another piece of good news is that since this work is normally paid according to a fixed and often flexible number of hours, this area is the least likely to get out of control and eat up all the time available. Admittedly, often PhD students don't feel they have a lot of choice here and must take whatever TA and RA assignments they can get. But look for ways to exercise agency, especially through the networking that we talked about above. There may be more flexibility and options than you assume.

Volunteer activities

We applaud any effort to make the world a better place and thus encourage volunteer activities in their own right. But make no mistake: Some volunteer activities can really help build specific competencies, knowledge, or contacts for your professional goals. This may mean getting involved in student associations, campus unions, and community organizations, or initiating things yourself where you see a need. (One option here is organizing alumni panels or employer panels for your department, allowing you to build competencies and networks at the same time.)

But be forewarned: The time demands of these activities may be bottomless, and the work can feel so needed and rewarding that you get sucked into making this your primary activity for diminishing returns. It is important to (1) set boundaries on time commitments and (2) look for opportunities that offer challenges and growth for you, or at least can lead to interesting stories to relate in a job interview. It's important not to lose sight of priorities here, lest you hear yourself saying things like, "I will only volunteer for the bake sale if I am put in charge of all revenues and addressed as chief pastry officer." But look for ways in which you can stretch yourself, build connections with your work and with other people, and generally make a difference both for the world and for yourself.

Employment

Some students seek out employment beyond TA and RAships during their programs. The primary motivation is usually income, especially after they exhaust their funding packages, and we certainly respect that. It's understandable, but the opportunity costs also need to be understood, since a job of any kind eats up time and energy and makes it harder to complete your program even if you are a little better off financially. (While some individuals can balance a full-time job with working on their dissertation on evenings and weekends, don't be certain you're one of them.) However, as with TA and RAships, the focus on income shouldn't negate a focus on building career competencies if at all possible. In fact, there are good reasons for taking a professional-style job during your PhD even if the income is not vital—as long as it advances your skills, contacts, and long-term prospects. You may even find it energizing to be in a professional environment (though see "eats up time and energy" above), and the closer the work is to your PhD interests, the more it might improve your dissertation. There are all sorts of possibilities here. It can be difficult to fine-tune things too closely (sometimes a job is just a job), but our message is that it can be okay to take on employment outside the PhD, though hopefully for career development rather than just a paycheque. It may even be that you enjoy it so much you abandon your PhD entirely (more on that below), which is also okay.

Our experience: Jonathan

In the fifth year of my PhD, I took a full-time contract for three months with the Ontario government. The project was on something closely related to my dissertation, it was a stimulating professional environment, and it allowed me to apply for full-time positions inside the public service. The work was interesting; I enjoyed every day, and it shaped a lot of my dissertation ideas and thinking. I never managed to land a full-time position, but if I had, I'd probably still be there.

Informational interviews

One of the best ways to learn about career options and what specific careers are really like is to speak to individuals who are working in a field. Informational interviews are a standard way to do this: They provide inside information and allow you to build and expand your professional networks. The idea of cold calling strangers to ask to meet with them may make you uncomfortable, but informational interviews are common and you should not feel that you are making an unusual or outrageous request. In the early years of your program, such meetings will provide you with key insights on the competencies that are valued in different careers; in the later years of your program, these meetings may lead to critical networks that feed directly into your job search.

Informational interviews in five easy steps

1. *Establish a list of 20+ names:* Brainstorm a list of people you know personally. Ask your supervisor, committee members, and graduate and department chairs for names of alumni from your program (both completed PhDs and those who left the program without completing) and from

other programs at your university. Ask your family and friends for suggestions, then move out to the true-strangers realm: Do a search of individuals with PhDs in your field, of names of individuals working in areas that might interest you, and so forth.

2. *Make the request:* Contact the person and ask for a short meeting at their convenience, ideally in their office (requests to meet "for coffee" or worse still "a drink" suggest an extended social engagement that verges on an awkward blind date). If the person is in a different city, request a short telephone conversation. Clarify that you are not asking for a job, but rather that you are seeking information on careers more broadly. The request should be fairly straightforward, such as the following email:

Dear Ms. Adams,

I am a writing to request a 20 minute meeting with you to learn more about careers in community relations. I am currently in the last year of my PhD in sociology and am curious to learn how community relations work. I am happy to meet with you in your office or speak with you by telephone at your convenience.

   Thank you for considering this request. I look forward to hearing from you.

Sincerely,

Melissa Abelson, PhD student

Department of Sociology, Bigcity University

3. *Prepare:* Do your background research. Learn as much as possible about the organization, field, and individual from online and other sources. Prepare a specific list of questions to ask about what the job type entails, what skills are involved, and what the entry points are. Include in that list of questions a closing question that asks if they can recommend additional people that you should talk to (and permission to use your interviewee's name when contacting said people). Ask frankly whether having a PhD is viewed positively or negatively in the field. You might be pleasantly surprised, but either way it is useful information.

4. *Work the interview:* Use the time as an opportunity to both gather information and develop your professional reputation and networks. Arrive a few minutes early (but not too early), dress professionally, and be respectful of the interviewee's time.

5. *Follow up and reflect:* Send a thank you email and keep a record for yourself of the date and details of the interview for future reference. Reflect on what competencies you learned to be valuable in that sector, and consider how you might build experience with (and concrete evidence of) that competency.

Our experience: Loleen

One extracurricular activity I pursued as a PhD student has had unexpected lasting benefits for me. On a whim, I signed up for an improv class. I had not taken any drama training before (or since, for that matter), but it looked interesting. The class taught me how to go along with things spontaneously in the moment and work positively with a situation that might not be what I wanted, how to respond quickly and effectively on the spot, and how to be comfortable in awkward situations. It was a fun activity that benefited both my think-tank work and my teaching career. (Live radio interviews, making presentations to decision makers, interacting with the public, and managing a large class of undergraduate students all require the ability to adapt in the moment.) It was an experience that paid off in ways I never expected.

How do I determine what is a sound investment of time?

As with everything covered in this book, it's not always easy to discern what the wisest choice is. So let's return to our guiding question: Given both my future goals and the information currently available to me, what is my best decision right now? This is particularly important when considering what additional activities to take on during your program, as you want to avoid time-sucking commitments with limited benefit. Thus, you need to weigh the amount of time required against the payoff you can reasonably expect. The questions in Table 4.4 will help.

TABLE 4.4 Worksheet: Assessing time vs. payoff

QUESTIONS	YOUR ANSWERS
Time:	
- Is this a fixed commitment or a one-time thing? Is it something I can get out of or adjust my involvement?	
- Is it short term (hours, days, weeks) or long term (months, years)?	
- Is the schedule flexible?	
- How likely is it that the time demands will grow?	
- What is my exit plan from this commitment?	
- How much research have I done on the above? How confident am I about my answers?	
Payoff:	
- What information, skills, or networks can I reasonably expect to gain?	
- Will this lead to a tangible experience or credential that others will recognize and value?	
- Do I view this opportunity as comfortably familiar, moderately challenging, or a great leap into the unknown? (moderately challenging = best)	
- Can I abandon this commitment without significant reputational consequences?	
- Is the activity likely to energize or drain me?	
- Does the activity involve any affiliations that may be problematic in any way? Or that may be beneficial in any way?	
- How certain am I about any of the above?	

Once you've answered to the best of your ability, think this way:

	LOW PAYOFF	HIGH PAYOFF
Limited, Flexible Time	If it makes you happy.	Definitely pursue.
	Things likely to fall in this quadrant:	Things likely to fall in this quadrant:
	- Some talks and events - Volunteer and paid work that does not build skills or expand networks	- Business skills workshops - Most career workshops - Most informational interviews - Selected talks and events - Selected conferences
High, Fixed Time	Avoid unless they provide needed money.	Pursue if you can, but double check all answers above first.
	Things likely to fall in this quadrant:	Things likely to fall in this quadrant:
	- Teaching and research opportunities that do not allow you to expand your skills - Heavy ongoing volunteer commitments	- Internships and other formal programs - Volunteer and paid work that allows you to build skills and networks

My side gig led to a real career opportunity. Should I finish my program?

Do you enjoy the career opportunity? Are you excited about it? If the answer is no, then deciding to pursue it—regardless of what you decide to do about your program—seems like a recipe for long-term unhappiness. True, a bird in the hand is a bird, but if you hate the bird its value to you is questionable at best.

But let's say you do enjoy the career opportunity, and you do see a future for yourself. The question now becomes this: Do you try to pursue both the career opportunity and your program at the same time, or do you have to choose between the two? Here again, some questions are in order: Do you enjoy your program? How close are you to being done your program? What are the costs (financial, personal, opportunity) of finishing? What are the costs of ending your program before you receive the PhD? Is the career opportunity in a field in which a completed PhD will have important cachet for you down the line (such as a non-academic university position or a research position of any sort)?

Some people can consider such questions with cool dispassion, but most people find these issues agonizing. They may have concerns about "quitting," feeling like a failure, letting a supervisor or a program down, giving up too early. Finishing the PhD may be a lifetime "bucket list" item, and they worry that its incompletion will haunt them. Before making any decisions, it is important to have a full understanding of your options. What are the possibilities for you to complete more quickly, working on a very concentrated basis? To complete more slowly, working on the program on a part-time basis? To switch dissertation formats to another available option? To change elements of your research project to make it easier to complete in a shorter time frame? To take a formal break from the program for a few months or even more?

Ideally, if you choose to leave your program, you will do so after fully considering all of the options and then determining that your drive for something else is greater. No matter what you decide, you want to be able to move forward with excitement and without regret. Take the necessary time to be able to reach such a decision point.

What do I do if I am at the end of my program and didn't do any of this?

There is still time. There is always still time. Let's get started right now:

1. Go back to the career competencies worksheet in chapter 1 and brainstorm both your program and non-program activities. Identify where you have concrete evidence and where you should make strategic investments of time and energy.

2. Look into the opportunities to complete a structured program, such as an internship. Assess if delaying your degree completion to participate in such a program is a worthwhile investment. Also explore opportunities for structured postdoctoral fellowships (see below) that integrate research and career training.
3. Identify the university programs and workshops that are available to you. Decide which present the most value relative to your current needs, and enrol immediately.
4. Set a target and timeline to complete 10–20 informational interviews. Ask your department for assistance in developing the list of interviewees.

Working your career means recognizing and maximizing your personal agency: You continually assess information and then make strategic choices in line with your goals. No matter what stage you are at, you have the ability to make strategic choices that can improve your possibilities and provide you with greater peace of mind.

How can I make the most of a postdoc position?

Postdoctoral positions have the advantages of providing a short-term career opportunity immediately after one's degree completion while allowing recent graduates to continue research engagement, expand professional networks, and increase their publications. At the same time, they are intended as temporary positions and almost always require physical relocation with the associated (and often high) financial and personal challenges of such moves. Postdocs are less institutionalized in the social sciences and humanities compared to the natural, applied, and health sciences, but they are still common and often highly competitive. Their exact nature will vary considerably in terms of duties, mentorship, research autonomy, and compensation in terms of salary and benefits. The single most common model in Canada in the social sciences and humanities is the SSHRC Postdoctoral Fellowships, in which individuals secure funds independently to work at a university other than the university from which they received their PhD. Most other postdocs are affiliated with individual researchers and units, who invite applications to work as a postdoc on a specific project (though the specificity varies), so the postdoc is essentially an employment contract with a specific individual scholar or research centre.

Just as you needed to show personal agency to work your program to maximize your career development, you also need to be strategic in how you work your postdoc. First, select carefully. If your primary goal is to build evidence of competencies for a non-academic career (including a research career), a fellowship that includes specific research training[3] or an employment-based postdoc where you work for a specific principal investigator on their project can be particularly appropriate. In considering these opportunities, seek out in advance clarity on the specific tasks and expectations for the position, and assess how these will aid your skill development and career positioning. If your primary goal is to become more competitive for an academic career, you should consider postdoctoral options that allow you to establish important research networks or add a prestige university name to your résumé and CV, and given the importance of Tri-Agency funding (discussed further in chapter 5), applying for SSHRC Postdoctoral Fellowships is important. And if you are applying for a second (or third) postdoc after already holding a first, you should carefully consider how you can ensure the new position gives you an opportunity to expand your competencies and broader employability, rather than simply continuing along the same path and buying more time in academia. Regardless of type, when applying for postdoctoral positions, review the eligibility terms carefully, as some competitions place a limit on the total number of times one can apply (in such circumstances, a premature application is particularly ill advised), and most place a limit on the length of time between doctorate completion and application.

Second, once you are in a postdoc position, actively show personal agency to deepen research and professional relationships, develop competencies, and publish. A postdoc where you collect the salary and mostly work from your home office is a wasted opportunity. Develop a strong relationship with your supervisor and actively seek out the training and mentorship that you feel you need at this stage of

---

3 At the time of publication (2018), an example of this type of program is the Mitacs Elevate postdoctoral fellowship. This two-year opportunity combines university research with a faculty supervisor and work at a partner organization, and includes a management curriculum to increase career skill training.

your career. Engage in the department community, and develop relationships with others beyond your immediate supervisor or research team. Set publication goals for yourself and use your time as effectively as possible (see chapters 6 and 7). And take advantage of your new university's career training opportunities, as discussed earlier in this chapter.

Third, make a decision immediately about where you are going to draw the line. In disciplines where postdocs are very common, it is increasingly typical to hold a string of postdocs before even being competitive for a tenure-track job. This is less the case in the social sciences and humanities, but for some individuals postdoctoral fellowships serve to delay an eventual shift to consideration of a broader range of career opportunities. Individuals holding a series of postdoctoral positions and limited-term appointments, with two years here and two years there, are not uncommon; for those who eventually end up in academic positions this gamble pays off, but for others there is an opportunity cost in that this time may have been better devoted to broader career development. There are many opportunities out there for you; perpetual temporary labour may achieve short-term goals but not your long-term ones.

How do I balance my program and non-program activities?

We began this chapter discussing the pop culture idea of going back and undoing regrets. As "do overs" are impossible, the goal is to minimize lost opportunities and unfortunate choices. In this chapter, we encouraged you to push your horizons beyond your formal program and seek out opportunities to increase your information, experience and skills, and networks. The career benefits are, we hope, readily apparent. But there are also personal benefits that may arise for you. Your engagement in the world beyond the academy will help make you a more interesting and relatable person. Generally speaking, people who do nothing but their jobs are boring, and this is even more true if they are academics. PhD students, having been taught to be critical thinkers and to engage aggressively with ideas, can at times lack a certain social awareness. They may not always realize when their demeanour is off-putting to a potential employer, colleague, or friend. Time in the broader world can help smooth out these social challenges that can arise from academic socialization. And, last but certainly not least, engaging in the larger world can be highly interesting and pleasurable. Life is short, and you should look for opportunities to enjoy it … even while you are pursuing your doctorate.

CHAPTER 5

ESTABLISH YOUR FUNDING TRACK RECORD

In his 1990 pop classic "Freedom! '90," the late, great George Michael sang, "Everybody's got to sell." Years later, Daniel Pink put forward a similar thesis (but without an accompanying music video featuring supermodels and a burning leather jacket, sadly) in his book *To Sell is Human* (2013). While the social sciences and humanities often consider the importance of framing and narrative, academia tends to discourage blatant allusions to sales and the idea of persuasion; there is often a prevailing sense that ideas and individuals advance purely on the basis of objective merit. This leaves those with a natural instinct for persuasive communication with a distinct advantage, and those clinging to the idea that "this idea speaks for itself" clinging just to an idea, with no actual funding for it.

Whether one is asking for funding, a job, or resources for their unit or organization, the ability to successfully make a persuasive case is a highly valuable career skill. Applying for grants and awards is a perfect opportunity for you to develop this ability and increase your comfort in acting as your own agent by making a case for yourself. Further, grants and awards are an external marker to the outside world that others value your research—value it so much, in fact, that they will devote money to it. And, of course, this is all in addition to the basic advantage of having financial support as you complete your program. So, given your need to develop the skill of creating persuasive cases to allocate limited resources for a particular cause, and given your need to, well, eat and pay rent, when you consider our overarching question—Given both my future goals and the information currently available to me, what is my best decision right now?—applying for grants and awards is easily a good choice. There is so much to gain that we are going to jump right in.

What is the difference between a grant, a fellowship, a scholarship, and an award?

These terms may be used interchangeably. A *grant* is typically funding provided to an individual (or team or institution) that is not repaid (unlike a student loan, a line of credit, or worse, credit card debt). *Fellowships* and *scholarships* are both types of grants. There are some fellowships out there that do not have funding, offering prestige and profile alone, but typically this is not the case. *Award* is an even more slippery term; typically, awards are things given *after* research or an activity is completed, such as awards or medals for the best dissertation, journal article, or book in a given year, but sometimes funds are given *during* the research process that are called awards. Some awards carry cash value, while others involve prestige and a nice certificate for your wall but no actual money. (Another entity to quickly mention is bursaries, which are awarded partly or entirely on financial need criteria, but they're outside our focus here.) As the language used is imprecise, we use the term "grant" for any scholarship, fellowship, or award that provides research funding at the start or during a research program, and the term "award" for any honour that is given (with or without money attached) to a completed activity.

What is a funding track record, and why do I want one?

Throughout this book, we have encouraged you to take steps to position yourself for a number of career opportunities, including but not limited to academia; we have repeatedly encouraged you to set your goal as a successful, rewarding career that uses your talents and the skills you developed throughout your education. Creating a funding track record—that is, a record of external grants and awards—will help you achieve this goal. Grants and awards provide future potential employers with a clear indication that your research is seen by others as meritorious and valuable. For careers in general, grant writing and generally pitching for opportunities and money is an important skill. And if you have any interest whatsoever in an academic career, you should be applying for grants and awards—note that we used the plural forms—because hiring committees are looking for evidence of research potential, and external funding provides one indisputable form of such evidence. Overall, a funding track record is increasingly a necessity for competitive academic job applications and may be a distinct advantage for applications in other sectors as well.

There are more immediate benefits to you as well. Constructing competitive applications requires you to cultivate your ability to explain your research in a compelling manner. The capacity to describe your research in a manner that excites others, answering the "so what?" question, speaks to your communication skills. Moreover, it is often in describing your research to different audiences that you start to notice areas for improvement in your work (holes in your argument, gaps in your literature base, limitations to your methodology) that you can address as your research evolves.

As many applications are not successful, applying for grants and awards provides you an opportunity to build comfort with risk taking and rejection. Many PhD students are accustomed to success; PhD students become PhD students because they were successful under-graduates and then successful master's students. Experiencing failure is an uncommon experience; you might have received a lower grade on a paper than you expected, but actual failure may have been rare. The problem with this continued success bubble is twofold: You might unconsciously stay within this comfort zone and avoid things that risk failure (and thus avoid the associated rewards with such things), and once you wade into publishing (see chapter 6) and into the job market (see chapters 8 and 9) you are going to need to get used to rejection. Applying for grants and awards helps you develop a thicker skin early and learn to be reflective about why you did not succeed so that you can make the necessary adjustments for future success.

And finally, the obvious advantage of grants and awards is money to support you and your research. If you already have external grants, there is a chance that you may be allowed to hold multiple grants at once. Even if you are not permitted to do so (and look into that carefully before assuming you cannot), you can use the *offer* of the grant on your résumé or CV as evidence of your ability to secure funding. It is better to list that you had to decline funding due to all of your other fabulous funding than to not apply.

Bottom line: Apply for grants and awards, even if you have other funding, even if you have sufficient employment income, even if you have a trust fund, and even if your partner or a family member claims to be "happy" being your sole supporter for a few years while you pursue your intellectual dreams. Keep applying throughout your program. Individuals are always striving for ways to distinguish themselves in competitive employment markets, and a funding track record is a great way to do so.

Our experience: Loleen

I applied for a number of grants and awards during my doctoral program, sometimes successfully, sometimes not. When I began my career, I quickly found that my past work in applying for funding was relevant to (and valued by) the not-for-profit I worked for. I soon was asked to assist with, and then eventually take responsibility for, writing grant applications to governments, philanthropic foundations, corporations, and other entities. Every potential funder had different information needs and required a specific "tone"; when looking to put together different funding sources for the same project, I was required to adapt to meet the needs of the audience, playing up certain aspects, providing varying levels of detail. My experience in applying for grants during my doctoral program provided me with the starting foundation that I built upon during my 10 years in the not-for-profit sector. I learned as much from my failures as I did from my successes, and it benefited my career.

When should I start building my funding track record?

In an ideal world, students start to build their funding track record as soon as possible. One can imagine the mythical strategic student who starts applying for grants and awards in the first year of her undergraduate program and then continues amassing honours small and large throughout her undergraduate career, pauses for a year as a Rhodes Scholar (of course), moves on to apply for a prestigious master's scholarship, and then for an even more prestigious doctoral scholarship, turning down Opportunity A in favour of even more lucrative Opportunity B. If this was you, congratulations, and we encourage you to be humble about such efforts to avoid alienating others. For everyone else, the time to start learning how the research grant world works and to start applying for grants and awards is now. It is not too late. It is possible that some (perhaps many) ships have already sailed, but it is just as likely that opportunities continue to exist for you.

Once you have identified an opportunity, aim to start working on your application at least two months in advance of the deadline. This lead time allows you to develop multiple drafts, solicit feedback from others, and generally polish your application for a greater chance of success. It also allows your nominator or referees (assuming you require such letters) time to develop strong, targeted statements of support that are informed by your application materials, rather than a generic "I taught Sally two classes and she wrote a good paper in each" letter that will not help your case. (See below for how to get the nomination letter you need, and chapter 8 for how to get the reference letter you need.)

At all stages, to be sure, pay careful attention to eligibility requirements; for example, some grants only allow you to apply a specified number of times, so you need to be strategic in when you choose to apply. But making the decision that you will make yourself aware of the opportunities out there, and then devising a plan to take advantage of them, is a good place to start.

How do I learn about grant and award opportunities?

Grant and award opportunities fall into two broad categories. The first are awarded to you with little to no effort on your part. (Sweet!) For example, your graduate program may automatically award scholarships based solely on grades; you may be required to submit a transcript, or they might just manage it on their own. Similarly, your department might submit all or a subset of completed dissertations to your disciplinary association for consideration for a best dissertation award. For such opportunities, there is not much you can or should do to advocate for yourself, other than sitting down with your supervisor and your graduate chair to find out what the opportunities are and to politely indicate you would appreciate being actively considered for anything that might be available. Departments can vary in the clarity and format of how such awards are allocated; in some cases, it's just up to the graduate chair to pick deserving candidates every year, and it is not unheard of for awards to not be given out because they are simply overlooked. Overall, there can be value in general networking and making sure to leave no stone unturned, but at the same time it's not always clear how much agency PhD students have for these types of awards.

Our experience: Jonathan

One day as a newish assistant professor, I opened up an email and discovered my book, based on my dissertation, had won an award as "book of the year" from an international research group that I really respected. Not only had I not applied for the award, I wasn't even particularly aware of it, and I am still not exactly sure how my book even got submitted. But it was a really meaningful honour that I am proud of, and it continues to look good on my CV. I was very fortunate that someone else was looking out for me, because I wasn't paying attention.

Our experience: Loleen

The unexpected emails I have received include spam and a mildly threatening hate email in response to an opinion editorial I wrote. Jonathan's experience is not typical.

The second category of opportunities are those for which you have greater agency, in that you are able to apply for them directly or through your program, providing a written program of research, CV, or other supporting materials that you can refine and tailor for the opportunity. You can imagine awards and grants as being on a ladder: The bottom rung contains those solely based on grades and past performance, and as you move up the ladder your agency increases because the importance of pitching yourself and your specific research grows. Your goal should be to aim to move up the ladder, building your skills.

To identify opportunities in this second category, you will want to undertake your own research, considering travel scholarships and awards (such as the Fulbright Program), government awards and grants, and private awards and grants. Because universities vary greatly in the amount of information they provide online, visit the graduate faculty webpages of numerous universities; this list should include your own university (or, if you are not already in a program, any university to which you plan to apply), other doctoral universities in the same province (as many funding opportunities are province specific), and then some from large, research-intensive universities in Canada. (If you are in a program outside of Canada, adapt these categories as needed.) Across the graduate faculty webpages you are sure to notice considerable overlap, but you may also find opportunities present on some sites that are not on others. Beyond this, conduct basic searches for opportunities specific to your discipline and topic, speak directly with your supervisor and your departmental graduate chair, and attend any research funding workshop offered at your university or by your disciplinary association.

Why are SSHRC grants such a big deal in Canada?

In Canada, arguably the most important grants are from the Tri-Agencies, which are the three federal academic funding agencies: SSHRC (Social Sciences and Humanities Research Council), CIHR (Canadian Institutes of Health Research), and NSERC (Natural Sciences and Engineering Research Council of Canada). Tri-Agency funding is important to universities, not just individual faculty; while the formulas and arrangements change over time, a significant portion of university funding is based on how well the university's researchers do at securing Tri-Agency funding. Universities typically receive an overhead amount as a percentage of each grant, allocations of other national awards are based on Tri-Agency success, and provincial funding formulas to universities may consider Tri-Agency funds among the metrics for fund allocations. The stakes, in short, are high, and many universities place clear expectations on faculties, departments, and faculty members to secure such funds because the initial grant is a foundation for so much more.

For social science and humanities students and scholars, SSHRC is by far the granting agency of interest, and for this reason we will focus our comments on this agency. Academic job candidates who have a SSHRC funding history, be it a master's scholarship, a doctoral scholarship, a postdoctoral fellowship or—ideally—all three, can be particularly competitive in academic job searches. Due to the institutional incentives for Tri-Agency success that ripple down to the departmental level, departments are keenly interested in a candidate's future prospects to obtain Tri-Agency funding when hiring for academic positions. A candidate's demonstrated ability in securing such funding as a graduate student or postdoctoral fellow is thus seen favourably. Other awards are also viewed favourably, but typically they do not have the prestige or the long-term Tri-Agency value implications of SSHRC awards.

How do I make my grant application competitive?

With grant applications, you are competing for limited resources. The adjudication committee has a finite number of grants to give out, and you must persuade them that your proposal is not just meritorious and meets the grant criteria, but also worthy of being selected above other meritorious applications that also meet the grant criteria. To be persuasive, you must appreciate and respond to the perspectives of others, see the world through their eyes, and identify how your work meets their needs. Essentially, you need to frame and position your work in the manner that suits them, rather than what makes sense to you. Achieving all of this requires three things: (1) a deep understanding of the grant criteria, (2) a compelling case that your work is worthy of being selected over other worthy projects, and (3) time.

Grant criteria

The grant information page will provide you with details about what types of projects and scholars are eligible, the adjudication process, and technical criteria. All of these must be taken very seriously. If you are ineligible, you should find something else to apply to, obviously. But look carefully at the purpose of the grant and the evaluation criteria, as these give you important strategic clues about how to position your work. Be bold and explicit in stating how you meet these criteria. For example, if the criteria are originality, significance, and feasibility, address these points directly:

- My project is original because x.
- The research question is significant because a, b, and also c.
- My research plan is feasible because [your training/planned training], [your access to data], and [your realistic timelines].

The adage "show, don't tell" is intended for fiction writing, and your grant proposal is not—or at least should not be—fiction. Tell explicitly, and then provide evidence to support your claims (tell, then show). As you work to explicitly address the criteria, you will at times struggle to make a strong case. This realization is good, as you can then do additional research or make additional refinements to your project to fix the deficiencies. Your research program overall and the grant application will both benefit. Finally, address the technical criteria. If the application requires you to use 12 point Times New Roman font, for goodness sake pay attention to this and make sure you comply! Failing to meet all of the technical criteria may get your application disqualified (all of that work lost because of your dedication to APA citation style!) or at the very least will make you look sloppy in your work.

Compelling case

Many grants—particularly those higher up the ladder rungs—require you to include a program of research or study plan. To succeed in these competitions, you need a clear narrative: a specified research question, a link to existing scholarship, and a plan of study (feasible methods and a timeline) that demonstrates how you will answer the question to build upon and advance that existing scholarship. Once you have outlined this information into a functional draft, you then need to revise it to make it compelling in the eyes of the adjudication committee. Your goal is to excite reviewers with the potential impact of your research, and the high likelihood that you will achieve this impact. As you revise your first and then your second draft, try to put yourself into a reviewer's mindset. Imagine a reviewer who is not a specialist in your subfield or even your discipline. Aim to impress them with your clarity, not your jargon and ability to use fancy words or drop big names. And as you revise, always look for ways to increase the energy in your application: Consider using the first person, kill all forms of passive voice, and find compelling verbs.

Time

The benefits of starting early on grant applications cannot be overstated. Starting early allows your ideas to percolate and evolve, and allows you to practise your ideas on different audiences for feedback, improving your ideas iteratively. As you read the second point above, you may have noticed that we mentioned writing multiple drafts. We recommend that you aim to never submit a first draft; ideally, you will have an initial draft, then receive feedback from a number of sources, and revise your application in response to this feedback. In working out your timelines for the application, double check the submission deadlines with your unit and university graduate faculty, as individual universities may have internal deadlines prior to the funding agency deadlines.

How can I be competitive for SSHRC doctoral funding?

Your personal ability to access highly competitive SSHRC funds varies at different stages in your academic life. (We should further note that there are different levels of SSHRC doctoral and postdoctoral funds, varying in competitiveness, prestige, and dollar value, but the general processes are largely the same.) One immediate point is that, at the time of writing this book, most SSHRC doctoral opportunities can

TABLE 5.1 Worksheet: Clarifying your work's significance

QUESTION	CONSIDERATIONS	YOUR ANSWER
In one sentence, what is your research question or objective?	This sentence must make sense to all audiences. If you cannot successfully explain it to the grocery cashier, your dentist, and your hair stylist (assuming they are willing to listen to it), keep revising.	
Why does this work matter? How will this work help society? How will it advance theory?	Just because it is important and obvious to you does not mean it is to other people. Why should tax dollars be used to fund this as opposed to (idealistic vision) medicine for sick children or (pessimistic view) large gala events to celebrate government achievements?	
How is your work original?	Demonstrate not only that you know the research area but also that your approach is original in some way; be explicit that the question is not answered by previous research and that you aren't just proposing to repeat previous research in a different population or time frame. If your research is just "adding to the pile," your grant application may be moved to the bottom of the pile.	
What evidence is there that you will be able to complete this work?	Being overly ambitious can be risky; while you want to generate excitement, you also need to instill confidence that you will be able to get the work done. Provide a realistic timeline and a compelling case that you have the necessary training and data access to see the project through to success. Feedback from experienced researchers is invaluable here.	

be won either at the start or in the middle of your program. Indeed, your program may require you to keep applying every year that you are eligible as a condition of your existing funding. This is a huge gift to late(ish) bloomers who may not have outstanding records or really clear research plans upon entry, but really shine in the first year or two of their programs. It also reduces the arbitrary timing of funding if your PhD entry cohort includes Genius A and Mastermind B, both of whom win scholarships that you would otherwise be a contender for.

Check the SSHRC procedures carefully, which change over time but have mostly gone in the direction of devolution except for the most prestigious scholarships and fellowships. Applications that were once all sent to Ottawa for national adjudication are increasingly handled solely within universities, faculties, and even departments themselves, with most universities given a quota of scholarships or a certain number they can nominate. SSHRC applications are infamous for their tight word requirements while being reviewed by broad disciplinary and multidisciplinary committees, putting a special premium on being able to articulate both depth and breadth at the same time. Strong applications use every word with care. Ensure your referees have your exact plan of study, so that their references can amplify and extend your own points. And, as we noted in chapter 2, application deadlines are typically well before the regular admissions deadlines, meaning you must be an early bird to have any chance of enjoying what is considerably more tasty than a worm.

Do not be discouraged if your SSHRC application does not succeed; rather, inquire how you might strengthen it for subsequent years (and for other types of competitions). Grades are typically the single most important factor in decisions, but by no means the only one. Review with your graduate chair or others involved in the various levels of adjudication how you might do better next time. They may be able to offer some useful insights or show you examples of successful applications that will inform your thinking.

Typical grant and award criteria

Calls for grant and award applications typically include at least some mention of adjudication criteria; though it may be brief or buried in the text, a careful reading may give you some great guidance on how your application will be assessed, especially for individual specialized grants and awards. Figure 5.1 shows one set of examples.

Typical Questions

A GRANTS JURY MAY ASK

WORKABILITY
Is the project realistic? Is the plan reasonably clear? Is there a clear sense that timelines can be met? Are there substantive risks or obstacles that might reasonably impede the project?

RELEVANCE
What is the connection to the subject of the grant? Does it answer important questions and/or shed light on important aspects? What does it tell us that we don't already know?

QUALITY
Is the project of clear merit? Are the proposal and methodology sound? Does the project promise a clear advance in scholarly and/or expert understandings of the field?

BUDGET
Does the budget appear appropriate and clearly connected to the project? Could the bulk of the project still proceed without funding (i.e., is it connected to specific costs or is it just a nice amount of money to have)?

TRACK RECORD
Does the applicant have a strong background for the study (e.g., academic excellence, previous research)? Do they have a strong record of achievement relative to their stage of career? Do they show promise and an upward trajectory?

FIGURE 5.1: Typical questions a grants jury may ask

How do I ask someone else to nominate me for an award?

Here is the perfect world: You open your email to find a surprise notification; you have been selected for the distinguished Great PhD award, or as a top 30 under 30 (or 40 under 40, since 40 is the new 30) award, or some other honour. You had no idea you were even being considered! Was it your supervisor who nominated you? Or your department as a whole? You are so touched and grateful; all this time you were quietly toiling away, they did notice!

We do hope this happens for you. At the same time, we want you to take whatever reasonable steps you can to strengthen your CV and résumé. And if this involves awkwardly asking someone to nominate you for an award, so be it. The fact that your supervisor or anyone else has not nominated you for any given award does not mean they don't think you are worthy of the award; it is equally possible they are unaware of it or just busy with other things.

Here is how to proceed:

1. Identify all awards for which you might be eligible. Read the criteria numerous times to make sure you are in fact truly eligible, both in personal (level of study, citizenship, etc.) and project terms, keeping in mind that while the former are usually fairly fixed, the latter may be more flexible. Pay particular attention to disciplinary language and terminology to ensure you actually understand the broad parameters of the award and are on the same wavelength as the funders. At the same time, don't rule yourself out too quickly, as the parameters may wax and wane over time, especially depending on who else applies that year. If you think you may reasonably qualify, and the work is not too onerous, it is worth a try.

2. Write up in bullet form a list of the award criteria and all of the ways you meet the criteria. Use clear evidence and elegantly worded sentences. This document will serve three purposes: (1) it will clarify in your own mind that you are both eligible and a worthy nominee; (2) it will create a case to your potential nominator that you are a worthy nominee; and (3) your potential nominator can use this document as the starting point for their nomination on your behalf.

3. Set up an in-person appointment with your potential nominator. Come to this meeting prepared with print documentation that provides full information about the award (including deadlines, addresses, forms, etc.), your case for your nomination, and any other documentation that might be needed for the nomination (such as your CV or a copy of your work). Impress your potential nominator with your professionalism, organization, and background work, and make it easy for them to complete the nomination for you. Do not worry about overwhelming them with information (within reason); rather, worry that they will complete the nomination without a key document or piece of information that you didn't tell them about.

4. When requesting the nomination, state clearly to the potential nominator that you are seeking the nomination because you feel the award would be beneficial to your long-term career prospects,

and ask if they would be able to provide a *strong* nomination on your behalf.

5a. If the person agrees to provide the nomination, ask what additional steps you could take to reduce the associated workload for them, and offer to follow up a week before the nomination is due to see if there is any assistance you might provide at that time. After the nomination is submitted, provide the nominator with a gesture of thanks, ideally a handwritten note or card rather than just an email or passing comment. If you receive the award, drop by to give them a second (yes, second) thank you card. It is hard to be too appreciative.

5b. If the person declines to provide the nomination, thank them graciously for considering the request. Reflect thoughtfully on why they might have declined, and consider if there is someone else you could ask to provide the nomination.

6. Regardless of the outcome of your request, and regardless of whether or not you receive the award, be proud of yourself for being proactive in trying to find ways to build your CV and résumé and for taking a risk.

Our experience: Jonathan

For several years, I was responsible for a student essay contest for the best paper about "Parliament." It was meant in a political science definition of the institution itself and its procedures and reform. Yet every year we received a wide range of papers on topics that went well beyond the above definition. Some were clearly ineligible because they were about political issues that, while they may have been *discussed* in Parliament, were not actually *about* Parliament as an institution. Such submissions were a waste of everyone's time, submitter and reviewers alike. But some papers were more on the edge, not primarily focused on Parliament itself but discussing other aspects of the political system (such as political parties) with clear references to the relevance for parliamentary institutions. They sometimes won depending on the quality and quantity of the overall pool that year. Ensure you are reasonably on target before you start applying, but sometimes you don't need to be exactly in the centre of the target.

How can I learn grantsmanship from a faculty grant application?

Usually the best way to learn is by doing, or at least watching others do it. This certainly applies to research grants, by which we mean watching faculty as they compete for grants themselves. Ideally this will be a valuable way to learn how to do it yourself, but the opportunities will vary considerably.

We mentioned in chapter 3 that there is no Supervisor School, so most PhD supervisors replicate their own supervision experience as the only model they really know. Similarly, faculty tend to replicate their own past experiences with grants when it comes to involving graduate students in the process of application and competition. Most grant applications are unsuccessful, so for obvious reasons most faculty are inclined to not tell grad students (or anyone else who doesn't need to know) about what they are up to unless it succeeds. But even when they do successfully obtain the grant, it doesn't occur to most faculty to let grad students know how it was done, and it is even less likely to occur to graduate students to ask. We encourage you to ask faculty (nicely) about the process of their successful projects, whether they could share their winning applications with you, and how they planned and targeted the application—all while explaining that you are trying to learn as much as possible about the art of asking for money as part of your long-term career development prospects.

In more fortunate situations, you may be lined up as a potential research assistant or team member on an application, and while your input may not really be solicited, you have multiple chances to watch and learn as the application takes shape. Take advantage of those chances (and, using your judgment, look for ways to contribute). Ask why certain things are done (or not done) and what the team thinks the strong and weak spots are in each draft. And whether the application is successful or not, ask to discuss possible reasons for the outcome.

What do I do if I am at the end of my program and didn't do any of this?

As we said earlier, there are numerous reasons to establish a funding track record, and the financial gains are not the most important among those reasons. As you approach the end of your program, your goal is to create evidence that demonstrates you understand the grant game—both the art of grantsmanship and pitching for money and the more general picture of how the grant world works in your discipline or area of interest.

Here are some steps you can take:

- Research what is out there that you can apply for as an individual student or scholar. Use this research time to educate yourself on the research grant world; be sure to have a solid understanding of SSHRC's various programs and criteria, but also learn about other government, private, and not-for-profit/ foundation funding options.
- Attend any research grant seminars that your university offers (how to write a grant proposal, how to create a Canadian Common CV, etc.)
- Let your supervisor and committee members know you are looking for experience with grant development, and ask if there are faculty members who are working on grant proposals who you might be able to assist.
- Organize a panel session on grant funding for new graduate students, inviting faculty and graduate students who have successful grants to serve as panelists.
- Conduct online searches on how to write successful grant proposals, even if you are not applying to anything in the near future.
- Look for ways you can develop evidence of your ability to write grant proposals and present compelling cases for funding through your extracurricular activities. It may be that your tennis club is applying for a community grant, or that you can take the initiative to find and pursue funding opportunities for your musical theatre group.

Above all else, be sure to maintain your own sense of personal agency; take the initiative to seek out opportunities or, if possible, to create opportunities for yourself.

How do I get comfortable with all of this?

Selling an idea—that is, getting people to buy into the need to support a project—is a skill set. Yet while this is a necessary skill for all of us, many academics are uncomfortable with the very notion of sales. They may associate sales with shady behaviour and with slick advertising campaigns. To all of this we say: Get over it. As your own agent, you must take steps to act in your own interest, and this requires understanding its importance and taking steps to develop this skill. It is a tool that will prove extremely valuable in your life ahead.

And now, assuming that we have successfully sold you on this idea, we will move on.

CHAPTER 6

BUILD A STRATEGIC PUBLISHING PORTFOLIO

In academia, the importance of "publishing" (inevitably defined as traditional scholarly journal articles and books) is often expressed in terms of volume and measurement: "I got five publications out of my dissertation"; "the applicant has a book and two articles"; "this is a mid-ranked press"; "the article has a high citation count." There is constant pressure, particularly for junior scholars, to score higher and higher on these measures if they wish to succeed in academic careers. Over time, publishing expectations have steadily risen, so everyone tries to publish more and to score higher on these measures to get ahead of those expectations—and each other. The result is a publication arms race. And no one really wins an arms race.

In this chapter, we suggest a different approach that defines publishing more widely and as part of a broader portfolio of your skills and competencies, rather than just having more than the next person. Project management and writing are fundamental parts of the PhD experience, especially in the social sciences and humanities. Luckily for you, each is also a key career competency: The world needs people who can take a project from idea to implementation to conclusion, and good writers who can communicate complex ideas and research into intelligible form. Publishing is a key mechanism to both develop and demonstrate these skills. The process of publishing is an education in itself that will benefit your career, and the product of publishing— that is, published work—demonstrates your ability to see projects through to completion, work with others (coauthors and editors), adapt to feedback, and communicate ideas effectively to external audiences who, unlike your dissertation committee, are not obligated to pay any attention to them. It is the evidence that demonstrates your ability. For this reason, you should plan to deliberately craft a strategy to develop a publishing portfolio that will support your claims about your project management and writing abilities, rather than just an arms race that you must win.

Do I really need to publish during my PhD?

Absolutely. You gain important skills in publishing that will make you more hireable both outside and inside academia. There are, of course, different types of publishing; we are limiting our definition to writing that has been reviewed and approved for public dissemination by someone else playing an independent editorial role. This can be in print or electronic, through a traditional commercial or scholarly publisher or an online editor, and really by anyone other than you or someone you are paying to "publish" the work. Work that has been reviewed for editorial quality and that has passed a firm test—publish it or not?—carries an external validation that personal online posts or your aunt's self-published memoir does not. As an aspiring career professional, your publishing time and energy should be focused on work that has been validated by others.

In order to simultaneously position yourself strongly for numerous career opportunities (discussed further in chapter 8), think about developing a publishing portfolio that crosses formats and speaks to different audiences while drawing upon the same project and knowledge base. Peer-reviewed scholarly publications are the coin of the realm in academia and can (sometimes) have value elsewhere. For academic jobs, it is rare to get hired without existing peer-reviewed publications, leading to the arms race discussed above. But whether or not you aspire to an academic job, your portfolio should also incorporate other forms of written communication—such as short media opinion pieces ("op-eds"), articles, essays, and reports—as such publishing can be valuable outside of academia and are increasingly valued within academia as well.

A tougher question is how much and where you should publish. Again, we return to our guiding question: Given both my future goals and the information currently available to me, what is my best decision right now? Your time and energy are limited, and you want to make strategic publishing choices that create the portfolio you need. More is not always better, and quality, visibility, and impact all count. "Scholarly" publications take the most effort and have varying cachet, but there is also a risk in generating lots of easier but minor outputs that do not add up to much, suggesting you can dash something off quickly but questioning your bigger substance.

So yes, absolutely publish. But make careful choices, and make them count.

What should I publish on?

While the academic publishing arms race is ultimately all about *how much* you publish, our approach urges you to think as well about *what* you want to say and to whom. Where do you want your ideas to resonate? What impact do you want your work to have? In the long run, this is what will give you satisfaction and, particularly for non-academic employers, is typically more important.

As a PhD candidate, you have a dissertation that will hopefully be publishable in part or whole. But perhaps more importantly, you have a dissertation *subject* and *expertise and knowledge* in it. You may also have expertise and knowledge in other areas, say from your master's work, or other things you are doing while working your program, though as we say below, this is the time to focus narrowly for impact rather than going off in multiple directions. This should be the start of your publication journey—having something to say and the competency to say it, rather than seeing everything only as chunks of material that will increase your volume count. (This is sometimes known as the "salami-slicing" approach of cutting research results into slimmer individual portions that can each yield a separate publication.)

You don't have to say everything, of course. We say again that publishing should be *strategic*—writing things that add value to and impact your career. Some publishing can actually have diminishing returns, if you say the same thing over and over, select poor venues, or take on projects that eat up time but don't really challenge you. Not only does this detract from other important tasks like completing your dissertation, attending a networking event, or spending time with loved ones, but too much low-level or repetitive stuff can suggest this is the limit of your ability and aspirations. Be alert to diminishing returns. As we will soon explain, it is important to keep focused on a single topic, so don't keep chasing new directions. To build your reputation in a particular area, you may need creativity and novelty to ensure you are building value while publishing on a tightly focused topic. And to demonstrate your ability to write for different audiences, it is also important to try to diversify your writing outlets.

Are book reviews worth the time?

Scholarly journals in book-oriented disciplines are always looking for people to write reviews of recent books. While of service to the profession and gratifying to authors ("Someone read my book!"), this can be time consuming and of limited reward to the reviewer. Many PhD students see it as a first step on the publishing ladder, but it really isn't. It is hard to write a truly good review, and readers will not remember who wrote it anyway—but the author will if you say anything they find overly critical. There's not a lot of upside, but there are definitely a few downsides.

Should I publish from my dissertation before I defend it?

There are two kinda-sorta-good reasons to *not* publish from your dissertation too early. The first is that it takes time away from the goal of completing the dissertation itself. But as you know by now, we don't advocate a single-minded focus on completing the dissertation at all costs. Publishing can even speed things up by helping you focus from a new angle. The second is that dissertations and the research behind them can take time to take shape, and waiting might allow you to produce much stronger publications in the long run—especially if you are in a book-oriented discipline that normally expects dissertations to be published as monographs. But waiting two to three years after your defence to hold your published dissertation in your hands in book form might not be helpful for your career goals. And if you head in a non-academic career direction, chances are good you won't publish your whole dissertation anyway, and you will have missed the opportunity to publish your work. Short-term gain and immediate gratification are good here, because your goal is to build your profile, advance your project management and writing skills, and get jobs and opportunities, and your publishing should serve that end.

Of course, some dissertations don't really break up into publishable chunks, so you might have to wait for the book. But most have at least one chapter, case study, or other piece of original research or reflection that can be turned into a peer-reviewed journal article. (Note that we specifically stated *journal article*. You want a proper refereed journal article if at all possible, because that appeals to potential employers and future hiring committees more than a chapter in an edited book. We will come back to this.) Consider the options available to you, and reflect on what best aids your career goals.

Should I publish on topics unrelated to my dissertation topic?

The challenge in working with ideas is that new topics are always so pretty, so tempting. Later in one's career, it can be delightful to explore new ideas, tackle them, and be open to new things. This is not the case, however, when one is in graduate school.

Ideally, all of your work, from your course papers to your dissertation to any additional papers that you write, will focus on a single topic. In practice, you might find you need to explore a few (ideally related) ideas before settling on one; you want to be sure that the topic is feasible and that you can access the necessary data and make a unique theoretical contribution before you commit all of your publishing eggs to one basket. But after you are sure you have a viable topic, it is a good idea to keep a narrow and disciplined focus on it.

Focusing on a single topic, as opposed to a number of somewhat linked or (worse still) different topics, works best for a number of reasons. First, with every new topic that you examine, there is a new literature, or two, or (for those venturing into the sometimes frightening waters of interdisciplinarity) three, four, five ... Mastering those literatures starts as thrilling and ends as being a lot of time and work. Simply put, it is more efficient for you to find a niche and develop it. Second, with every item you write that focuses on the same theme, you build your external profile in the area. Two or three pieces on the same topic can add more credibility than five pieces on different topics. Third, every time you focus and expand on the same theme, you build your own internal competence on the topic. Much has been written about "imposter syndrome," the pervasive sense that everyone else out there is highly competent whereas you are just faking it. It is not a good feeling to believe that you are out of your depths. It does not feel good to believe that you only know the surface literature. Avoid it.

Where should I publish?

Regardless of your career goals, you should pursue scholarly publishing in some form during your PhD, and we will devote most of our discussion in this chapter to that. But in addition, we urge you to build your publishing portfolio by adding selected non-scholarly publishing. There are numerous opportunities to write for key non-academic audiences, such as industry publications, practitioner journals, and so forth. You should seek these out. Writing for these outlets allows you to learn how to write for different audiences (an important skill), and then provides you with evidence for potential employers and granting agencies that you can, in fact, write for a range of audiences. The publications allow you to increase your profile outside academia, which may help you to build networks (discussed further in chapter 7), while inside academia they are increasingly valued as part of knowledge mobilization. And such publications, often more so than academic publications, can have influence on ongoing debates and even practice. Such influence is both professionally and personally rewarding.

When deciding where to publish, variables to consider include the following:

1. The purpose of the writing: Is it advocacy? Reports and analyses? General interest or entertainment?
2. The audience: Is it the mythical "general public"? Enthusiasts or professionals interested in a narrow field? Decision makers?

3. The style: Big words? Data driven? Anecdotal? Simple and accessible?

4. Who initiated the writing: Are you responding to an open call for submissions? Were you approached to do it? Were you specifically commissioned to write something?

Any combination of these could be valid ... or not. Beware the thirst of many outlets for content—any content, it seems, as long as they don't have to pay for it. Sometimes, though, a publication may not have many readers or impact, but is still a mark of quality and a career-advancing move because you were asked to do it (many government reports fall into this category). We caution against publishing primarily for the sake of advocacy except on topics squarely in your area of research expertise; when you do publish advocacy pieces, be sure to make it about *analysis* more than opinion. The bar is often low here, and some outlets are always looking for quick opinions on controversial subjects, but resist the temptation to publish your opinions on matters in which you may be an informed and engaged *citizen*, but not a research authority or expert. We are not against saving the world, but we urge you to focus your time and energy strategically.

A publication can range from a few hundred words to tens of thousands (or more, in which case it's called a book). This usually correlates to time commitment, though much depends on how much work you need to do before you sit down to write. It also correlates somewhat to impact and influence, but with more variance. A 700-word op-ed at just the right time on the right subject can advance your standing (and demonstrate your responsiveness and nimbleness) much more than 5,000 earnest but only modestly relevant words somewhere else. However, short writing usually only has a short burst of impact. Ideally you should look for both sprints and marathons.

You may well think at this point that this is all great, but this world of op-eds, public essays, and reports just doesn't apply in your field. Yet we believe strongly that in almost any discipline or field in the social sciences and humanities, *someone* is looking for *your* ideas and research in written form (though they may not have money to pay for it). Admittedly, few government departments or corporate boards sit around thinking, "we need to commission an analysis of references to polar bears in nineteenth-century Germanic literature," but organizations devoted to polar bears, the Arctic, or German literature might be interested in the aspect relevant to them. Sometimes the demand is certainly more obvious, but we urge you to take our above assertion as a given and think creatively about who that *someone* is. The first and best way is to consider the things that you read yourself. Can you see yourself fitting somewhere in there? Expand further to the wide universe of low-profile specialized publications, such as professional and industry journals, that have small but highly dedicated readers looking for engaging and substantive content. It doesn't need to be a perfect fit and is unlikely to cover *all* your areas, but we believe you will see places where you could publish. You can then consider whether it is in your strategic benefit to do so.

In all cases, when pursuing these publications aim to keep the topic within your area of expertise, as discussed above, and to maintain a professional tone, supporting your positions with evidence. Further, while these non-academic publications are a great *addition* to your writing portfolio, they should not be the entirety or even majority of your writing portfolio; be sure to pursue scholarly publications as well.

Should I pursue scholarly publications if I have no interest in an academic job?

Yes. While non-academic employers may indeed be indifferent to your piece in the *Journal of Very Important Studies,* it is rarely to your detriment (you are pursuing a PhD, so they already know you have suspicious scholarly tendencies) and it keeps your options open. A scholarly publication can still serve as a mark of prestige and a demonstration that you are able to complete projects, have some authority in a field, and can engage with other authorities as a peer. Scholarly publications are particularly valuable for quasi-academic and research-oriented positions where there may be no expectation you will conduct research of your own, yet it makes people feel good that you're published and thus must "understand our world." It also preserves your academic career options (something we encourage in chapter 8), since scholarly publications are critical to being considered seriously for an academic position.

TABLE 6.1 Assessing the strategic benefit of publishing opportunities

Will this primarily draw from my existing expertise and knowledge (including my current dissertation research)?	Existing: 20 points "In a way": 5 points No: −10 points
Will it be published in an outlet read by the people that I want to read it?	Yes: 15 points No: −10 points
What is the likelihood of acceptance?	Pretty good (it has been solicited or discussed with the editor): 10 points Crapshoot (most unsolicited submissions): 3 points Equal to being struck by lightning: −10 points
Money: Will I get paid for this?	Yes, big bucks: 20 points Yes, but not much: 7 points No: 0 points
Impact: What sort of impact/resonance do I expect from it? (Be honest.)	Pivotal and long term: 20 points Will add to general knowledge and debate: 5 points People will talk about it, but only for a week: 0 points Probably not much: −5 points
Time: Will the total amount of time to do this be measured in hours, days, weeks, or months?	Hours or days: 5 points Weeks: 0 points Months: −20 points
Leaving aside money and impact, am I excited about this publishing opportunity?	Totally: 12 points It's worth a shot: 3 points No: −10 points

Scoring (should I pursue this opportunity?)

Below 15	Never
15–40	Probably not. Go back and double your scores (including negatives) for money, impact, and time and see if your score significantly improves.
40–60	Maybe
Above 60	Go for it!

The good news is that writing a scholarly publication is perhaps the best education there is for understanding academic research. As you write, you are forced to condense your arguments and evidence into a specific word count, often 6,000–10,000 words, which focuses your writing style. This forces you to be very clear about your theoretical contributions and to state these explicitly and forcefully. The process also requires you to reflect upon and justify your methodology, and to acknowledge its limitations. While you can hide numerous flaws in a 300-page dissertation, a stand-alone article is so bare-bones that the problems of your research are easy to see. This sounds intimidating, to be certain, but once you have a draft article and can see these problems for yourself, you are in a position to address them, resulting in better research overall. The writing process also makes you a better reader and critic of other people's published research.

Writing a scholarly publication also forces you to push beyond writing for familiar audiences (your professor, your supervisor, your doctoral committee) to writing for strangers. It requires you to look at your work with a cold, dispassionate eye—just as a future human resources officer or hiring committee will someday look at your job application. Again, this can be intimidating and requires a certain degree of bravery. But it does get easier with time, and through the process you learn not only how to anticipate how you and your work are perceived, but also how to focus on what is and is not within your power. In academic journal article publishing, you will quickly learn to make the *submission* of the journal article, rather than the acceptance of the article, your primary goal: You have no control over whether the article will be accepted, but you do have control over whether you complete it and submit it, and over how you respond to the feedback you eventually receive. This lesson to focus your energy and attention on areas where you have agency carries over to applying for jobs in academia and in other sectors, and it will serve you well in the long run.

Are book chapters or journal articles better?

Journal articles.

Oh, sorry—you wanted more? While some disciplines certainly value *entire* books over journal articles, and both book publishers and journals vary enormously in quality, journal articles are on balance definitely more valuable than book *chapters* because (1) they stand alone as individual author-initiated submissions and (2) they (normally) depend on double-blind reviews where you don't know who the reviewers are and they don't know who you are. This stand-alone, arm's-length relationship is the gold standard of scholarly publishing. In contrast, and as we say in more detail below, edited books may be rigorously reviewed by editors and may go through a single-blind review with anonymous reviewers, but they do not have the same arm's-length relationship and stand-alone merit of a journal article. Journal articles are also more accessible online and in search engines, giving them greater visibility and potential impact. We talk about the strengths of book chapters below, but make no mistake: On balance, articles almost always have more career value.

How can I get a journal article published?

There are typically three main steps to journal article publishing, which are outlined in the following sections.

Step 1: Choose wisely

All journals display certain patterns and parameters, not just in disciplinary fields and subjects, but also methodologies, writing and organizational styles, and audiences. Your journal selection determines both the audience you are writing for and the article's structure (including length). The question of *how* to select your target journal can be complicated. Aiming too high for the top journals in your field can be risky as the chances of getting published are low; journal rejection can be crushing (we don't use that word lightly) to even the most seasoned academic authors, and the process takes time. On the other hand, you don't want to underplay your work by only considering the lowest hanging fruit. The best place to start, we suggest, is by identifying journals where the scholarly conversations in your niche area are occurring. For each, ask yourself, "Can I reasonably, truly imagine my article appearing in the journal and being of interest to its readers?" If so, the journal is a worthy contender.

Should I
SUBMIT TO THIS JOURNAL?

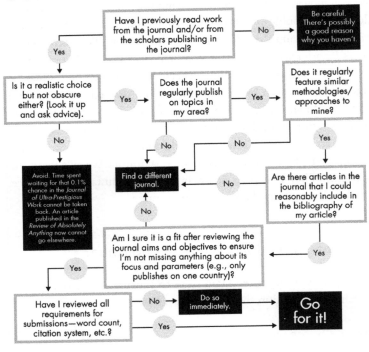

FIGURE 6.1: Should I submit to this journal?

What are predatory journals?

An entire shadow industry of predatory journals and vanity presses exists solely to "publish" academic work for a fee and allow people to add dubious entries to their publication list. While a few fall into a grey area between reputable and predatory, most outlets are obvious with their aggressive solicitations and "quick review and publication" promises. Publishing with these can have major reputational consequences, suggesting you are either naïve and gullible or you knowingly published in a disreputable location to pad your CV. Neither will aid you in reaching your career goals. The good news is that it does not take a great deal of due diligence to avoid these outlets if you do a little research and ask around.

Step 2: Create structure

Journal articles often follow a formula. This formula will vary according to discipline, methodological tradition, and sometimes even the journal itself, but if you study your target journal, you should see a general pattern. How long do introduction, literature review, analysis, and conclusion sections tend to be? Emulate the structure you see in the journal, particularly for articles similar in topic or method to your own. After it is written, have a trusted person help you proofread it and ensure that you meet the journal's style guidelines. Then, when you feel it is ready, send it in.

Step 3: Lick your wounds and move forward

Your submission is unlikely to be accepted on the first try (if it is, keep your lucky streak going and head to the nearest casino) and will likely receive one of two responses: rejection or revise and resubmit. Chances are also good that, regardless of which response you get, you will receive some feedback that seems harsh. It will sting. All of the voices in your head (at least one of which sounds like *that person*, your graduate student nemesis to whom everything comes so easily) will be quick to tell you that this rejection is a clear statement of your worth, your abilities, and your terrible, terrible choices. Your research question is boring and irrelevant, you should have used different data with better analyses, your work is theoretically deficient, and your writing is sloppy. Also, you could be cuter, or at least better dressed.

Rejection

The best thing to do with a rejection is to wait a few days. Once the worst feelings have passed (and they will pass), you need to assess the feedback. If you received a "desk reject," in which the editorial team decided not to send your paper out for review, consider if it occurred because the journal was a poor fit or because the contribution of your paper was unclear. Typically, the editor will provide you with a small amount of feedback about why the paper was not sent for review, but it is extremely limited (and frustrating). If you received a rejection based on the editor's assessment of the journal reviewers' comments, you have the advantage of peer feedback in the form of the editor's summary comments and the reviewers' detailed comments.

It is important to take the time to think strategically about your next steps. Unless you are truly convinced that the work should never see the light of day, make the commitment to rework the material and get it back out there. Keep your end goal in mind: an article that can be part of your strategic publishing portfolio. The only way to do this is to get your article back out and under review. Find a second journal to submit your work to, then ask yourself whether this journal is truly a good fit for your work, and if so, what changes are necessary to fit the journal structure and style. You also need to ask yourself if the merits of the paper are easily apparent to the editors and reviewers. If you have received detailed feedback, you need to assess which comments merit changes to your work, which comments suggest a misinterpretation of your work that require you to communicate your ideas more clearly, and which comments are best saved for rants to close friends about how terrible peer reviewers are.

In making these assessments, including the decision on whether or not to move forward with the article, you ideally will have someone you trust that you can discuss these matters with. Your supervisor seems like an obvious choice, but there may be other individuals who can assist you. Be sure to select someone who has experience with journal article publishing and who will provide you with constructive advice (as opposed to cheerleading or copy editing).

Revise and resubmit

If you are given the opportunity to revise and resubmit back to the journal, get to work on it immediately. Make yourself a schedule and establish a plan to do everything you can to address the reviewers' comments. It is helpful to create a table with three columns: reviewer, comment, response (see sample provided in Table 6.2). If a reviewer's comment is even remotely reasonable, try to find a way to address it. If it is not reasonable, try to find a nugget within it that you can work with. If it is completely unfathomable to you that any change whatsoever be made in response to the comment—and if you

TABLE 6.2 Reviewer response table example

REVIEWER	COMMENT	RESPONSE
Reviewer A	"I was not convinced that X leads to Y."	In the revised manuscript I provide the following two additional sources of evidence to support the claim that X leads to Y: ..
Reviewer B	"I am disappointed that the author has made no reference to the extensive work of Smith."	I have added references to the work of Smith, clarifying that her work applies to daytime while my focus is on night.

are certain, truly certain, that you yourself are being reasonable—then find some way to politely and respectfully explain why you are unable to accommodate that particular change.

The next critical step is to respond directly to the reviewers and to every single comment. If they write something flattering ("This paper is well written."), the response is gratitude ("I thank Reviewer B for this positive assessment."). If they recommend including a particular body of literature, explain how you incorporated this literature. You will send all of this to the journal editor along with the revised manuscript. The amount of detail you provide in this revision table may seem overboard, but it is necessary to demonstrate both to the reviewers and, more importantly, to the editor, that you have taken the critiques seriously.

Our experience: Loleen

When I was a PhD student, I sent a paper into one of my discipline's national journals. It was a sole-authored work and related (albeit not as directly as we recommend) to my dissertation topic. I received a revise and resubmit, which I now with hindsight consider to be an encouraging outcome. At the time, however, I was daunted by the work required to meet the reviewers' comments. My supervisor, to his credit, told me that I should resubmit, but I failed to do so within the three-month resubmission window. Looking back, I regret that choice. While the resubmission may or may not have resulted in a publication, I deprived myself of the learning opportunity.

Should I write a book chapter
for an edited book?

Maybe. Probably not.

   This is different from a sole or coauthored book, which in many disciplines is the highest goal. But edited books have a mixed reputation. There are field and methodological landmines here, as the format of stand-alone journal articles may seem to fit certain types of scholarship that are easy to break up and present in 8,000 words with no further context. Work that is more theoretically complex, interdisciplinary, or otherwise does not fit neatly into existing patterns in the field may be better served as part of a broader collection of similar chapters that together make a more coherent whole. Yet while edited books can be great things for scholarship, their career value is shakier. The above factors mean that book chapters inevitably have a reputation as repositories for work that isn't strong enough for a journal article, which as we said above will always have a higher rank because of its stand-alone processes. And many academics see book chapters as the jury duty of scholarly life: undesirable, but nearly impossible to turn down when summoned. Thus, while book chapters are not *bad* and may be the best way to publish particular kinds of work, they have definite risks and costs that may outweigh the benefits.

   One of the largest risks is time. The edited volume may never see the light of day, or may ultimately be published years (sometimes many years) later than the editors originally promised or hoped. Peer-reviewed journal articles typically have a quicker turnaround, and articles are often made available online far in advance of the actual issue date. Decision making in journals is also more straightforward. Though articles typically go through at least one round of revisions and can be at the mercy of slow reviewers, the article is ultimately either accepted (sometimes conditionally, with clear steps to resolve the conditions) after which it enters the production process, or not accepted. An edited volume, by contrast, will have several stages, even if you've been invited to contribute with the implicit presumption that the chapter is a sure thing. It will likely go through one or more rounds of revisions with the volume editor, followed by a further round of revisions through the publisher's peer-review process, and only then does the publisher make a final decision, which may be

influenced by commercial as much as scholarly reasons. If the project starts with a workshop or conference for contributors, that means
an additional stage of presentation and feedback, which is good for
the work, but it stretches things out even longer. Hence, promises of
a "forthcoming" book chapter are sometimes viewed by academic
hiring committees skeptically. Journal editors, required to make regular decisions, will also be more on top of the job than most frazzled
book editors (see below on why you should not edit a book at your
career stage). Opting to contribute your work to an edited volume
rather than a journal risks that the work may languish for years before
(possibly) seeing the light of day. In that time, the work could have
been published elsewhere, informing scholarship, amassing citations,
and building your own résumé and CV.

Nevertheless, there are benefits to a book chapter. They are scholarly publications after all, and being part of an edited collection can
be an invigorating experience. A cohesive and path-breaking book
can lead to more exposure than an isolated journal article and give
you opportunities to publish work that indeed does not fit easily in
journal article format. Participating in an initial workshop is especially
rewarding, as your work will receive far more attention and informed
criticism than any conference panel, and you'll have an opportunity
to meet and interact with other people in your field (ideally at all
stages of career). And a good book editor who knows your general
field and knows what they are doing will be a joy to work with and
make you a better scholar. Appearing in a good edited collection—
especially alongside some big names—makes you look good, and if
the book is a hit, more people will come across and remember your
work in the collection than the average journal article. Finally, as
mentioned above, the journal article format can favour some types
of scholarship over others. An edited collection can allow contributors to play to different strengths and tackle different theoretical,
methodological, and empirical angles as a collective, rather than
having to hit all the bells on their own. So book chapters definitely
have their merits, especially for new forms of research and interdisciplinary research. Having said that, at the dissertation stage, your
work *should* be hitting all the necessary theoretical, methodological, and empirical bells and hopefully can be published accordingly.
Book chapters are best left for later in your career when you want

to explore new areas and have the opportunity to be part of something bigger.

Our experience: Jonathan

For years I researched the politics of evangelical Christians in Canada, but I had much more success publishing this research as book chapters or in invited special journal issues than through stand-alone journal articles. A constant problem was that the topic straddled disciplinary and methodological boundaries, and existing research was very American-centric and difficult to build on either theoretically or empirically. This left everything very open ended without firm boundaries, and I struggled to package work into 8,000 stand-alone words that would satisfy reviewers. In contrast, edited collections provided a coherent overall framework in which my work could be one part of the puzzle, without needing to tie up every angle. But journal articles still would have been better for my career.

Should I edit or co-edit a book?

No. Editing a book seems like such an easy thing before you get started. In the shiny, optimistic vision that you can picture so clearly, the contributing authors will submit their chapters on time, at a high standard. You will develop important contacts with important people, and these relationships will advance your career. You will get to know publishers, who will be there for you when you are ready to publish your PhD dissertation in monograph format. Future employers will see the edited book among the many accomplishments on your CV or résumé and single you out for job interviews. And above all else, it will be easy and fun and just come together naturally. Plus your name will be right there on the cover, for all of the world to see!

We hope that our skepticism was evident in that last paragraph, but in case it was not, here is the reality: Editing books is a bad choice for pre-tenure academics generally and for PhD students in particular. As we have already explained in our discussion on book chapters, edited books are an uncertain business at the best of times.

You simply do not have the time to devote to uncertain, potentially stressful projects that do little to advance your publishing portfolio. Add to this the potential relationship costs (do you, as a graduate student, really want to be badgering a senior scholar about a chapter that is three months late?) and the advantages (if they existed) of editing a book evaporate.

If you still decide to go ahead with plans to edit a book, make sure to not leave yourself beholden to particular chapter authors (e.g., a book that includes a chapter on each Canadian province, with only one particular specialist available to write the chapter on Prince Edward Island). Your life will become hell.

Should I coauthor?

Probably, but (probably) not exclusively.

Norms vary dramatically by discipline (and even subfield) here, with sole authorship being the overwhelming norm in some disciplines but multiple authors being the custom in others. Relatedly, some disciplines have a strong expectation of supervisors co-publishing with their students, while in others this is exceptional. You probably already have a good idea where your discipline or supervisor fits on these scales.

If sole authorship is common in your discipline, we'll note that there are many advantages to working with a coauthor. First and foremost, if you work with a good supervisor or mentor who considers the coauthorship a form of career mentorship, you stand to learn a significant amount about scholarly writing and in a constructive manner. Second, coauthoring can be more efficient than sole authoring, allowing you both to build your publishing portfolio and to increase your profile as an expert in the area more quickly. Third, successfully coauthoring work provides you with evidence for future employment claims that you can work well with others. However, all this depends on finding a suitable collaborator. You may have little power over your supervisor's choice to coauthor with you. But you may find opportunities to approach them or another mentor with a specific idea. And you certainly have agency to seek out peers, especially fellow students, to work with.

On the other hand (though your discipline may have a different dominant view here), you should ideally publish at least one journal article on your own. You want to clearly demonstrate to future prospective employers that you are able to independently make an intellectual contribution, to independently complete work projects, and to independently write at a high-quality level. The use of the word "independently" in triplicate in the last sentence hopefully drives home the point that coauthorship can raise uncomfortable questions for prospective employers and creates undesirable ambiguity about your exact contribution and capability. If you publish with your supervisor or other mentor, a search committee or human resources director is torn. Did you do most of the work? Were you more a research assistant than intellectual collaborator? Or was it a genuine partnership of equals? It could be any of the above, and it is difficult to know. The questions may be fewer if you publish with your peers, where there may be a presumption of a more balanced relationship and genuine collaboration. But even here you have not clearly and irrefutably demonstrated your ability to work independently (yes, we used that word again).

If I do coauthor, how do I make it work?

Coauthoring can lead to almost any outcome: a highly positive experience, a highly negative one, or any point in between. In many ways, it is analogous to taking a road trip with someone: Even if you think you already know them fairly well, by the end of the trip you know far more than you ever expected to ... and in some cases hoped to. We could belabour this analogy by referring to disputes over who should drive, whether or not the passenger is contributing in a meaningful way, and whether the washroom pitstop was overly long, but as this will prove tedious, let's move on to some practical advice.

Successful coauthorship comes down to expectations and communication. When coauthoring, you need to pay attention to who needs (or wants) the publication more. There are power dynamics at work in most relationships, and that is true in authorship as well. Often, there is one individual who is more committed to and motivated by the project; this person might be the principal investigator on the grant funding the research, or a graduate student seeking to add to their CV. While you don't need to have an explicit discussion about the topic ("Mark, I feel I care more about our paper than you do ..."), in your own head it can be useful to clarify whether or not you are the driving force behind the work or not. If you are the person who wants the publication more, expect to do more (in some cases, almost all) of the work. Yes, this may seem unfair, but (hopefully) you are still getting something out of the partnership, such as strategic insight or data access, to make the coauthorship worth it. If you are the person who wants the publication less, you need to be careful that your lower motivation doesn't result in you failing to fulfill your commitments, thereby damaging the relationship.

Clear communication is key in coauthoring. The business adage of "underpromise and overdeliver" applies here. If you realistically think you can get the work to your coauthor by October 15, promise it for October 31; in the best case, you impress them with your efficiency, but if something comes up that pushes your schedule back you have some extra time to meet the deadline. Here we refer you to chapter 7 and suggest you build these coauthorship commitments into your schedule in a realistic fashion. If you find that the scheduling exercise leads you to conclude that you have taken on too much and cannot reasonably expect to meet particular timelines, let your coauthor know as early as possible, and if necessary offer to withdraw from or take a lesser role on the paper.

I am at the end of my program and didn't do any of this. What do I do?

As always, it is never too late. First of all, if you have completed or are about to complete your dissertation, start thinking about what you can do with it. Could it be published as a book? As a series of articles? While the process takes time, effort now could yield happy things later, and if you are interested in an academic job, scholarly publications are vital. In addition, review the first part of this chapter and the wide world of publishing beyond scholarly outlets. We remind you: Somebody somewhere is looking for your ideas in written form. While a scholarly publication has inherent value regardless

of your career goals, those goals may be better served at this point by looking primarily at other types of publishing that can emerge much faster and establish your professional credibility. And you can still work on that submission to the *Journal of Never Too Late Studies*, because that will also advance your goals. Publishing is ongoing, and once you get started, you will get in the groove.

So, bottom line, what should I do about writing and publishing?

We started this chapter by describing the publication arms race in academia. We urge you not to focus on somehow winning that race by producing more than anyone else, but to see publishing as a wider goal that spans different types of publishing and builds and illustrates your overall skills and expertise. We believe you should do the following: (1) start publishing during your PhD program; (2) focus on a select topic for which you seek to be known; (3) think widely about all kinds of publication outlets while prioritizing scholarly publishing; (4) be highly selective in your writing outlets and highly conscious of the opportunity costs of different options; and (5) consider coauthorship as a supplement to (rather than a replacement for) sole authorship. You will ideally leave your PhD program with a publishing portfolio that demonstrates your ability to complete projects, meet scholarly standards, work independently, write for diverse audiences, and contribute substantive information in your area of expertise. And it always looks great to see your name in print, and no one—arms race or not—can ever take that away.

CHAPTER 7

CULTIVATE A PROFESSIONAL REPUTATION

Indulge us as Generation Xers for a moment over a late twenti-eth century TV drama, ER. While the show had many memorable moments, including a new surgeon's parking lot fist pump after receiv-ing praise from a supervisor (something that should resonate with graduate students), there was a line repeated at numerous points over the series that influenced both of our careers: "You set the tone."

In chapter 1, we introduced the need to strategically develop career competencies. Among these was the nebulous category of profession-alism, which includes things such as the establishment of a professional image and time and project management. At this stage in your life, it is probably no surprise that how other people perceive you matters, and the need for time and project management skills makes itself quickly apparent to PhD students. Unfortunately, mentorship in these areas can vary, and the structure of PhD programs does not help. Once one gets past the coursework stage, it is possible—in fact, often far too probable—for PhD students to become socially isolated, reduc-ing their opportunities to carve out a professional niche. Moreover, preparing for comps and writing the dissertation are activities that lack a clear end point: One can always do more research, read more literature, tighten one's text. And time can seem plentiful, particularly if one is willing to work long hours in the evenings, on week-ends, and on holidays. When you combine these factors and consider the infamous Parkinson's law, which asserts that work expands to fill the time available, it is a recipe for potential disaster. In the PhD program, work will continually expand, just like the universe itself, complete with black holes in both cases.

Fortunately, all that flexibility means you have tremendous personal agency to identify both how you would like people to describe you and how you would like your daily life to function, and then to adopt strategies for achieving these outcomes. In this chapter, we introduce a set of practices to increase your efficiency and reinforce a personal brand that is associated with competence, conscientiousness, and general professional awesomeness. In addition to advancing your longer-term career goals, these practices can make your life better immediately. We will warn you, though, that many are outside what you typically observe in academic life, and you may feel resistant at first. Academia often cultivates an image of difference and separation from the rest of the professional world as well as a strong sense of individuality, so you may be tempted to believe that you have unique working habits and a style that only you really understand. While some things we suggest may not work *exactly* for you, we urge you not to play the "this doesn't apply to me" card over and over. As a scholar, you are naturally interested in evidence, so treat yourself as an experiment with a sample size of one. If, after a few months of reduced stress, met deadlines, and professors starting to treat you like a peer rather than a student, you truly feel the ideas are not for you, you can always stop.

How can I cultivate a professional reputation?

People described as being professional share a number of qualities. They are typically known for being reliable, conscientious, and attentive to detail. They understand the need for appropriateness relative to their circumstances and the importance of acting graciously. At its core, professionalism is largely about treating others respectfully in a broad sense. When you make the effort to be punctual and to ensure that your work meets a particular standard and that your behaviour is appropriate to the situation, you are showing respect for other people's time, energy, feelings, boundaries, and so forth.

You personally set the tone for being professional; it is entirely in your own hands. Cultivating a professional reputation requires taking small actions regularly to consistently demonstrate respect for others. What is often unappreciated is that failing to do so leaves other people with a sense that you *disrespect* them. This disrespect is almost always unintentional. But make no mistake: actions such as arriving at class a few minutes late, being unprepared for a meeting or interview, and failing to thank someone who has made an effort on your behalf are not just perceived as disorganization; they can be and often are perceived as a lack of respect for another person's time and energy. And over time, a reputation for being disrespectful can be deadly to your career.

Adopting three mindsets will help you avoid unintentional disrespect:

1. *Graciousness is not optional:* A lack of attention to gratitude will seal your reputational coffin if you are not careful. Always, always say please. (We feel we shouldn't have to write that, but sadly a shocking number of people at all career stages skip this basic human courtesy.) And, closing the loop, thank people when they do something for you, even if it is small, and even if they are your supervisor, instructor, or committee member. When people do things for you—share an idea or source, provide you with feedback—they are giving you a gift of their time and attention. As your parents undoubtedly taught you, failing to say thank you for gifts is unspeakably rude. People typically notice when they are *not* acknowledged for their efforts, and you can easily turn a potential champion into someone who has no investment in your success. If someone is helpful to or supportive of you, take the minute it takes to express your gratitude. If someone provides you with detailed feedback on your work, provide a more lengthy positive response (even if you don't agree with their comments). If you *intend* to say thank you but fail to actually *do so*, the person is left with the impression that their efforts are not valued by you or that you feel entitled, and that person will be unlikely to help you again in the future. (If someone needs to ask if you received the email of detailed comments on your chapter, you are almost certainly added to their "people who don't impress me" list.) Make it a habit to thank people within 48 hours, for all things large and small. Better that you have the reputation of being too polite and thoughtful than of being a jerk.

2. *Your department is your workplace, and the people in it are your colleagues:* After years in the educational system, it is easy to treat your doctoral experience as "more school." But to cultivate a professional reputation, you must show awareness that this is your professional training ground. While it is tempting to become casual and overly familiar with respect to language, clothing, hygiene, and social behaviour, it is not appropriate to the circumstances. Professionalism requires a strong sense of context, as well as respect for differences in power and authority. Here are some things to avoid: being late; showing up at meetings unprepared, without pen and paper or tablet/laptop and a clear purpose; profanity; discussions of illegal or illicit activities; sloppiness, be it in personal attire, non-proofread emails and materials, or data and file management; anything beyond light alcohol consumption. Save these behaviours for your private life (or avoid them entirely).

3. *All information is private unless you are told otherwise:* The move from casual student environments into the professional world can be difficult for PhD students, as information can be sensitive in multiple unforeseen ways. Conversations "just between us" are not always so, emails are forwarded, and information that seems benign may prove explosive. You need to become highly sensitive to showing others respect by developing a hyper-instinct for discretion. As a teaching assistant, you are privy to confidential student information; as a researcher, you may have access to data sets, draft papers, and similar things that are not meant to be shared. Sometimes it's crystal clear; other times not. Always err on the side of caution, asking if something can be shared (and even more importantly, explaining why it needs to be). And if you are gossiping or voicing opinions about faculty, other graduate students, undergraduate students, staff, or anyone else, know that it will get back to them or be repeated to someone else. If you wouldn't say it to their face or send it to them in an email, rethink voicing it at all.

How do I create a professional image at conferences?

Conferences can be critical for building impressions, good and otherwise. This involves your work and accomplishments, skills and competencies, general professionalism, and personality—roughly in that order. Conferences provide snapshots of you, and it's important to make sure the snapshots are accurate. Keep in mind that you are always "on," at least to some degree, and make the most of it. Anticipate certain questions and be prepared to summarize your dissertation, describe your research interests, lay out your professional roadmap, and, of course, highlight your key competencies.

It is important to figure out the correct norms for conference presentations and sessions. Professional-style conferences are typically more genteel and the questions are more affirmatory than critical. This is not the time to take apart the speaker's entire framework of ideas, and it's even okay to slip in self-promoting references to your own work. In contrast, it is generally considered polite at academic conferences to challenge the presenter's work; people expect to be grilled about their basic ideas and assumptions and even express disappointment that "I didn't get any good comments." Take advantage of this, but use it carefully. Make it about the presenter's work, not your own; the "statement pretending to be a question" is common but easily overused. Aim instead to ask questions that are constructive, that draw linkages to other work (not just your own), and that will promote interesting discussion in the room. You might be tempted to demonstrate your intelligence by aggressively pointing out the flaws in the presenter's work. While there is latitude for this even as a PhD student, there's also great risk of unintentionally creating an impression of being obnoxious. People may or may not have thick skins, but they always have long memories of times when they were publicly embarrassed. Given the smallness and interconnectedness of the academic world, there is no reason to make enemies, be it with an established professor or a fellow graduate student.

It is common at conferences to focus on Great Persons and try to interact with them. Fine, but a better investment than a one-minute forgettable conversation with an Eminence is time spent with ordinary mortals closer to your own world, including your own PhD peers. You might stumble into a serendipitous opportunity by talking to just the right person at the right time, but long-term connections are the big objective here. This can include having fun socializing, but being known as the party animal is not a good career move, whereas "one drink and then leaving" is not a bad reputation to have. And be attuned to the norms of conference dress codes, though this will vary. At professional conferences, dress like a professional unless you really want to stick out as the wooly-headed scholar. But academic conferences, especially in Canada, tend to be much more casual with a wide range from suits and skirts to hoodies and shorts. Our advice: Figure out the general norm and dress one level up.

How can I be productive?

Professionalism means doing what you say you will do and by when you say you will do it. You cement your professional reputation by getting things done—and done well, on or ahead of schedule. This requires the ability to manage time, resources, and energy to make this happen, over and over. By carefully managing your time and your projects, you will be more thorough, meet deadlines, and avoid accidentally missing steps.

Most productivity and time management tips are written for business audiences. The target reader works at a desk managing projects with clear, looming deadlines and has a boss who is highly interested in the worker delivering something (reports, analyses, new code, corporate strategies, etc.) by a specific date. No deliverable, no profit, and soon no job for the employee. These books tend to assume that the reader needs more time—sweet, uninterrupted blocks of time—to work on something with clear parameters and built-in boundaries.

PhD students face a very different challenge. While taking classes, you have various paper deadlines to balance and possible teaching or research assistant responsibilities. After classes are done, you are trying to coordinate reading literature with dissertation-related writing, more teaching or research work, a panel that you are organizing, and so on. But these responsibilities are typically done within a context of large amounts of unstructured time. The illusion of abundant time can be overwhelming, and the projects themselves get more challenging. Scholarly life is full of theoretical and empirical rabbit holes and blind alleys that can drain your time and energy. Again, dissertations in the social sciences and humanities lean toward the model of "go away and think," and students are provided with limited direct guidance and supervision. Not only is this a route to inefficiency and years of drift, it also undermines the building of professional habits and demeanour.

Deliberately building project management skills increases your prospects for career success. And like other aspects of professionalism, it requires careful attention. Fulfilling your project commitments, and doing so in a way that allows you to retain some degree of quality of life, won't necessarily happen naturally. Four basic steps that you tailor to your personal energy patterns and circumstances can ensure that you are achieving your goals while maintaining quality of life.

Step 1: Make a list of what needs to be done

Quite often, people try to just keep everything straight in their heads. The problem is that it is easy to forget things or to remember them inaccurately. The solution is simple: To determine what needs to be done, you need to get organized by writing a list of everything you have committed to and the associated deadlines.

"Wait," you might be saying, "this is rather obvious." Of course it is. But just like "eat right and exercise" is obvious but frequently ignored advice for healthy living, the practice of listing commitments and deadlines remains a habit that many PhD students have yet to adopt. If you have already done so, good for you: You have our full permission to enjoy a well-deserved sense of self-satisfaction. For our more mortal readers, let's get down to business. Start with a large "brain dump" of commitments for a specific time period. (The academic semester is a good place to start.) Are you taking classes? If so, check each class syllabus and then list all of the readings, papers, exams, lab projects, presentations, and other class tasks, noting the associated dates. Are you working as a teaching assistant? Again, check the class syllabus and list all of the class tutorials, exam dates, paper dates, and other TA-related responsibilities and their dates. Are you working as a research assistant? Working on a conference paper? Do you have committee responsibilities? Other responsibilities that we have failed to mention? Do your best to think of everything you have to do over a specified time period, and then scan both your calendar and your email to see if there is anything you have missed. The more complete your list, the better. List complete? Excellent. Now just reorganize the list by due date and you have a clear picture of what needs to be done.

What do I do if I have taken on too much?

Feeling overwhelmed is awful. The panic in your chest, the feeling that you are going to let people down, that you will need to do nothing but work and more work for weeks or months, the associated anxiety and insomnia .. It is the worst. And the fears that are associated with it are often well based:

If you are someone who fails to meet commitments, who is constantly behind on timelines and long on excuses, it reflects poorly on your professionalism. At a certain point people may start to perceive you as either unreliable, incompetent, or both.

If the amount you have on your plate is not realistic relative to the time available, you need to identify where you can make changes. Are there any committed times that could be reduced? Is working fewer hours in your part-time job, or getting help with family responsibilities, or reducing commute times an option? (You may be tempted to cut back on sleep, fitness, or personal hygiene. Please don't.) Chances are good that your ability to make change in the committed time part of the equation is quite low. So then you must ask, are there any projects on your list that you don't really need to do at this point in time? Or are there some steps within the projects that can be removed or streamlined?

Ideally, you can solve your overload problem well in advance: You can tell people that you will need to decline a particular opportunity for now, or that you will need to have someone work with you to complete it, or that you will do it for a later deadline. These conversations can require a certain degree of bravery, but it is better to be upfront with people as early as possible rather than disappoint or anger them at a later stage. On the plus side, the discomfort of disentangling yourself from overcommitment may serve you well in the long run as you instinctively avoid taking on too much in the future.

As we have said at several points in this book, be attuned to your mental health and wellness. Seek balance and support networks; check in regularly with a counsellor or other source of assistance. Everyone feels stressed and overwhelmed sometimes; learn to ask for help in identifying when it is too much, and seek the support you need.

Step 2: Break activities down into smaller tasks, distinguishing between high- and low-energy tasks

Start with the list that you created in step 1. Now look carefully to see how you can break the items down into discrete tasks. For example, the paper due on October 31 requires numerous individual steps to complete it: creating an outline, searching the library database for relevant sources, reading these sources, writing a first draft, editing the draft, writing a second draft, completing the bibliography, and so forth. This detailed list allows you to create target completion dates to keep you on track and, importantly, to manage your time and energy strategically.

When you look at the more detailed list, it should be apparent that some tasks (such as writing, reading, or data analysis) must be done when you are at your peak, and other tasks (such as editing a bibliography) can be done when your energy levels are lower. By clearly labelling tasks as high or low energy, you can strategically assign the high-energy tasks to those time periods during which you are usually highly productive, creative, and energetic, and assign the low-energy tasks to the times when you are usually a bit spent out. (At this point in your life, you probably have a good idea of which times are which for you; if you are not sure, just pay attention to your energy levels for a few days.) Your goal is to protect your high-energy periods for high-energy work, and restrict all low-energy work and other activities (like dental appointments and coffee meetings) to low-energy times; to do this, you need to clearly label the tasks.

Step 3: Block work time into your calendar

The trick to getting things done (and done well and on time) is to schedule the work times into your calendar and to respect these times. Remember, an unstructured schedule and its illusion of endless time

TABLE 7.1 Worksheet: Tasks, target completion dates, and energy designation

TASK	TARGET COMPLETION DATE	ENERGY DESIGNATION

is your enemy; imposing structure on your days is necessary. Doing so is simple:

1. Block off all committed times (classes, work hours, commute times, sleep, fitness, family responsibilities, etc.) in your calendar.
2. For each task and project, estimate the number of hours you will need. Because most things take longer than you assume, and to provide cushion in case of unanticipated events (illness, transit strikes, broken water heaters, etc.), increase this number by 50 per cent.
3. Working back from the deadline, schedule task-specific working time in your calendar, assigning high-energy tasks to the high-energy time slots.

Now, in doing this process, you may be prone to optimism ("I don't need to increase the project hours. My original estimates are realistic."). We understand. But imagine—just as a thought exercise—that we are right that things tend to take longer than anticipated and that life sometimes throws curveballs. Blocking the extra time into your calendar allows you to quickly identify if you have taken on too much and then make needed adjustments. Of course, if your original estimates are accurate, there is risk of turning down opportunities that you could have completed. For this reason, we suggest that you treat the thought exercise as just that. But if your gut is telling you that you might have taken on too much, respect that and proceed cautiously.

Be strategic in how you enter things into your calendar. It is imperative that you save your high-quality times for high-quality tasks. The most important thing to schedule is your writing time. Social science and humanities doctoral programs involve a lot of writing: Most courses involve written assignments, and after courses are done there is (in most traditional programs) the dissertation proposal, the dissertation itself, and other writing that you seek to complete. Writing should therefore be paramount in your schedule, and we strongly suggest regularly scheduled short writing sessions (e.g., every Monday, Wednesday, and Friday from 9 to 11 a.m., or every Monday to Friday from 1 to 2 p.m.). This approach, admittedly, goes against the typical academic binge-writing style, in which the author procrastinates and then completes all the writing tasks within a large block of time, like a second-year student cramming for a final exam. To be sure, there can be a time for binge writing. But like binge eating and binge television watching, it has both short-term satisfactions and long-term consequences, and inevitably the former exceed the latter. Regularly scheduled writing may not fully eliminate the need for occasional binge writing, but it can reduce it (and the associated stress) dramatically.

To make the best use of high-energy time, you need to consciously batch together low-quality tasks (e.g., getting books from library, checking citations and bibliographies) and commit to addressing them *only* during low-energy periods in the day. Email in particular can suck up time and energy with little payoff. Make a decision to file email into a batch folder that you will address at a prescheduled low-energy time; during your high-quality work times respond only to email that, if not addressed immediately, may result in someone bursting into flames.

How can I take advantage of unexpected time?

Most weeks include a fair bit of relatively useless time. Sometimes this time is structured into your schedule (commuting time or time sitting on the pool deck while your child takes a swim class) and at other points it is unanticipated (time waiting outside your supervisor's office because his department meeting is running long). Sometimes it can be good to just stop, take a breath, and relax looking at online cat videos (so cute!). But sometimes it is nice to make use of this time, and you can plan ahead for these opportunities by ensuring your writing projects are accessible through the mobile device you are undoubtedly carrying. The three-minute note here and the five-minute idea there will actually add up to paragraphs, and the perennially growing file creates within you a sense that the project is moving, while eliminating the frustrating "start up" time that can occur if you don't work on a project regularly. If you adopt this practice, you will start to see small windows of time as bonus time. A friend is late to meet you for coffee? Great, you can edit your introduction! Your child has a 30-minute gymnastics class that you sit through every Monday night? Awesome, you can aim to write 150 words each time. This approach needs to be tempered; you should never feel that every second must be used efficiently. But if you can tackle some tasks during found time, you can free up more time for other things in the future. Which, we must stress, could include a run by the river, or beer with a friend.

Step 4: Work your calendar

Ah, plans. Like fitness schedules and New Year's resolutions, making them is the easy part. But the execution, well, that takes discipline. And this is where the difference between the professionals and the others shows itself.

Scheduled writing is often the most challenging commitment to keep—which is ironic, since this single activity is most associated with a PhD student's success (or lack thereof). Honouring your scheduled writing commitment as much as you would honour a class, meeting, or other work obligation is the sign of a true professional. But it can be hard: While thinking about writing is exhilarating, and reflecting on completed writing is satisfying, the in-between period—you know, the actual writing—invokes a broad array of emotions, not all of which are pleasant. As well, the more theoretical and interpretive your work is, the more likely it is that writing is the primary or even sole activity itself, as opposed to gathering and analyzing empirical, documentary, or archival data and then writing about it, making writing even more paralyzing.

Many writing problems occur because people are trying to plan, write, and edit simultaneously. To get around this, start with a clear outline and then focus your daily efforts on small units within the outline. Allow yourself to put ideas in point form, making notes to yourself in the draft to be dealt with at a later time (e.g., "insert three to four sentences about Jones et al. here," "add citations"). Avoid the temptation to edit as you go along so that your creative thoughts, which will generate the innovative ideas that matter to your work and your discipline, are not impaired by your more critical editorial thoughts. Aim to get a full first draft completed before you turn to editing the work. The more you focus on small sections and just getting ideas down, the more your writing time can actually be allocated to ... writing.

Working your writing time—treating it like the heart of your job—is key to your professional success. It can be tempting to schedule something else in the writing time slot "just this once," or to fail to use the time wisely when you are in it. And it can be tempting to use low-quality tasks as "short" breaks during your productive periods ("this paragraph isn't really going anywhere … I'll work on my passport renewal form"). Remember that tasks expand to fill the time available, and the task might end up killing your productivity for the day. The small writing time investments add up to significant results. And the more frequently one does something, the easier it becomes, as both the runner and the smoker can attest. Use the power of habit and routine to your advantage. To further your progress, consider establishing a writing group that provides support and creates a sense of accountability.

Our experience: Loleen

One thing that can be helpful in meeting writing goals is an accountability system. Within my first year of returning to academic life, I set up a writing accountability group with six other female tenure-track professors. We came from a variety of academic disciplines but shared a similar tenure timeline. The group met monthly for two years and was fundamental to my progress. Knowing that these peers were aware of my month's goals helped motivate me to push forward on my writing when other things seemed more pressing.

Making it a practice to repeat these four steps will develop your professional image. You will get projects done on time, giving others the sense that you are on top of things and take your work seriously. People will notice that you are organized and competent, and they will respect you for this. Plus, you will have time to join them for a squash game or coffee.

How do I communicate professionally?

Many people believe themselves to be great communicators because they find it easy to articulate and express their thoughts. But this only counts if people are receiving and absorbing the information as intended. Communication is not about you—it's about the people to whom you are communicating. It incorporates courtesy, discretion, and respect for others' time. It also requires understanding that not everyone views the world like you do or thinks and processes information the same way. Your quick efficient message may be seen as terse and rude; your effort to explain all of the facts may come across as an eye-glazing monologue. The failure to appreciate how others might reasonably process what one is saying is the cause of many misunderstandings and tensions ("Oh, no! Here comes Dr. Longwinded") and undermines many otherwise professional people.

Our experience: Jonathan

A practice I have always tried in my professional career is to listen and communicate with people on their own terms, in ways that resonate and make sense to them and how they process information. Early in my career I knew an academic administrator who was very well liked, and people often raved about how easy it was to talk to that person. I also respected the person, yet our occasional conversations were awkward and stilted. Eventually I realized that we had the same technique of letting the other person set the pace of the conversation, and were waiting for each other to take the lead.

Professional communication encompasses the principles that we have talked about already—respect, discretion, sense of appropriateness—while effectively sharing information. What many people don't recognize is that communication is about the other person. If the other person misinterprets or misunderstands the information you are attempting to convey to them, you need to figure out how to alter your communication style to meet their (and ultimately your) needs.

Many universities have resources and services—housed in libraries, teaching centres, research offices, and graduate faculties—available to help graduate students develop their skills in packaging and presenting ideas. It is also helpful to simply watch other people's communication styles carefully and to consider what you find effective. Give careful

TABLE 7.2 **Professional communication**

DO	DON'T
✓ Include a proper salutation ("Dear") and valediction ("Sincerely," "All the best," etc.) in all email and written communications.	✗ Address a stranger or person with higher professional status than you (e.g., professor, potential employer) by their first name until you have clearly been signalled to do so.
✓ Pay attention to how people you regularly interact with process information, and adapt your style accordingly.	✗ Barge into people's offices unannounced with a "quick question."
✓ Spend 5–10 minutes carefully composing your question or written communication so that the recipient can understand (and, ideally, act) within 5–10 seconds.	✗ Forward emails without permission.
	✗ Make complex requests of people when they are clearly distracted or limited for time.
✓ Devote more time to listening or re-reading the other person's communication than you do to responding. Ask questions and restate information to ensure clarity.	✗ Respond to emails when you are in an emotional state (good or bad). If the fire in the belly is telling you that you have to send that email *right now*, step away from the computer or put down your phone.

thought to the professional tone you want to set, and seek out real-life examples of people to emulate.

How can I network effectively?

A great deal of opportunity and influence comes about because someone knows someone else, or someone knows someone who knows someone, and so on. The academic world itself is densely interconnected, and academics are often good at networking with other academics. But as we suggested that your goal be a successful, rewarding career that uses your talents and the skills you developed throughout your education, we encourage you to expand your networking beyond academic circles. While interacting with individuals beyond academia can require a bit more effort, it is in your interest to do so since, as we note in the next chapter, many career opportunities are not advertised. As you build your networks, you increase the number of people who are in a position to suggest your name when one of their contacts mentions they are looking to hire someone—the "weak ties" we talked about in chapter 4 that can be vital to employment networks. Think of your professional network as a sphere of concentric circles, and constantly be aiming to push out further (see Figure 7.1).

Networking takes many forms. It often has a strong social component; thus, many professional events and receptions are explicitly labelled "Networking Opportunity," in case anyone wasn't clear. But it also includes one-on-one meetings (such as the informational interviews that we discussed in chapter 4), email contact, connections through social media, and any other way you bring your professional abilities to another's attention and vice versa. Some people over-network—they treat every encounter as a transaction, flood others with updates ("just wanted to mention my book review got published and here's a copy"), and give the feeling that every contact is just

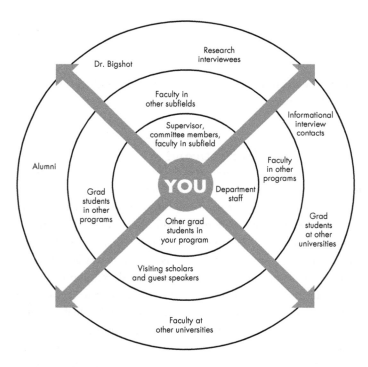

FIGURE 7.1: Expanding your professional network

a stepping stone to a more important one. But the more common problem is under-networking. PhD students can be particularly prone to this because they are typically more introverted than the general population, and academic culture emphasizes modesty and understatement. Many PhD students get the message to let their work do the talking, and thus do not cultivate the professional skills of connecting and building networks, to their own detriment. Networking can appear superficial, because some of it is. But, for better or worse, it is how people get to know each other and decide if there is professional value to the relationship.

Networking also requires effort. This may mean going to things you don't really enjoy and striking up conversations with people you don't know, or spending time calibrating an email to ensure it says exactly what you want it to say. It also means thinking and planning ahead. Are there specific people you want to talk to at an event? Are you targeting the right person with your message? What do you want them to learn about you? What information would you like to learn from them? In some cases it may require writing down and memorizing talking points beforehand to ensure you get a crucial message to a crucial person right. Take pride in being prepared.

As a PhD student working your career, you hopefully have a number of professional attributes and angles to fuel your networking, but the big one will be your dissertation, which (hopefully) showcases your main interests and abilities. So it's important to be able to talk about it in ways that make sense, both inside and outside academic circles. Take advantage of competitions that require you to summarize your dissertation in a few minutes, and develop further mini-versions with hooks that pique people's interest, making them ask for more ("You've uncovered the theory of the universe? Please continue.") Similarly, you should develop equivalent summaries of your skills and competencies. Be able to speak convincingly and confidently about what you can do and why it is relevant and valuable. You set the tone. You're a professional.

How can I use social media effectively?

Professionalism is timeless, but its tools change, particularly the use of technology. Navigating this change can be a challenge, especially as conventions evolve around the boundaries between the professional and personal. A person dropped into our present-day world from the twentieth century would be shocked to learn that seemingly professional people would freely post random personal thoughts that could be viewed (and archived) instantly by anyone in the world. The twenty-first century person, on the other hand, may be surprised to learn that it was once common for faculty members to list their home phone numbers on course outlines, often with a gentle reminder to not call after 10 p.m. Boundaries and expectations change, and not always in one direction. There is a general evolution in society toward more openness about personal lives, which is often a good thing, but there are always limits.

The online world gives you ever more tools to express yourself both personally and professionally, and you need to decide how those two relate. We urge you first to keep at least some boundaries and privacy controls between your truly personal life and everything else, so that no potential employer will ever see an image of you in a bathing suit. Beyond that, you have agency to decide how much you want your professional online brand to be animated by your personal style, and which online platforms provide the best opportunities to do so. The one important thing is consistency. The online brand you show to the world (different than what you show family and friends) should give people confidence in your abilities and your judgment, rather than making them wonder about your professionalism.

Using social media and similar online tools is a professional skill in its own right, though many people overestimate their talent here. Simply posting lots of content that people respond to is not necessarily a sign of anything; it can even be detrimental if it's not backed up by other online or offline accomplishments that demonstrate you do more than live on your phone all day. If social media skills are something you want to demonstrate as a skill set, you need to show clear planning and evidence of your effectiveness.

I am at the end of my program and didn't do any of this. Where do I start?

This is our closest thing to a life skills chapter, as professionalism is a lifelong quality and there is no reason why you can't start becoming more professional today. We said above that academia can be a terrible place to develop professional skills, especially for productivity, and we are utterly confident that many of your peers are struggling with these issues as well. It may take time to unlearn bad habits of productivity and develop good ones, but you can become steadily better at interacting with people and developing confidence. Nobody was born a professional. They developed into professionals, and so can you.

And, of course, it is never too late to go back through your publicly accessible social media feeds and remove anything that may be viewed as unprofessional.

These ideas are interesting, but how do I actually make them work?

Professional reputations are built one interaction at a time: If you are selectively or sporadically professional, you will not be setting an overall tone. Knowledge of your occasional lack of professionalism—missed deadlines, poor communication—will eventually start to creep into your professional reputation. This means that professional behaviour, including time and project management practices, must become a habit to be effective.

We have been advising that you continue to ask yourself the question, Given both my future goals and the information currently available to me, what is my best decision right now? As we said at the start, professionalism is about setting an overall tone, and it is in your interest to start setting that tone immediately. No one is perfect, and professionals are inevitably stronger in some of the above things than others. But it is the overall tone—that sense of reliability, conscientiousness, respect for others, and graciousness—that pulls things together. There will always be loose threads, weak points, and sometimes a paralyzing embarrassment as you suddenly forget someone's name at the worst possible moment, but if you focus on setting the tone, it will keep propelling you forward.

CHAPTER 8

LAUNCH YOUR CAREER

Decades ago, Dale Carnegie wrote the classic business self-help book *How to Win Friends and Influence People* (1936). The book was translated into numerous languages, and Carnegie's ideas continue to be taught in leadership training programs. While his stories may be dated, at least one of his ideas is highly relevant as you explore moving from PhD program to career. That idea is simply this: To influence people (e.g., to influence them to consider you seriously for a career opportunity), it is critical that you think of what *they* need and want, rather than what *you* need and want. If you can position yourself as a solution to their problem, you have a better chance of achieving the outcome you desire.

The principle of being a solution to someone else's problem is essential when approaching the job market and exploring career options. Organizations—whether big or small, in the academic, private, public, or not-for-profit sector—do not hire people for the sake of hiring them. They hire people because they have identified a need, a gap—a *problem*—and at least part of the solution is to hire someone to solve it. Similarly, successful entrepreneurs flourish because they identify a problem, along with the solution to it, that others will pay to resolve. As we stated in chapter 7, you set the tone; you have the agency to frame yourself professionally. As you transition from student to career professional, you need to think carefully about how you can position yourself as someone who can be the solution to a prospective employer, client, or customer's problem.

Throughout this book, we have returned you to a single question: Given both my future goals and the information currently available to me, what is my best decision right now? We suggested that your goal should be a successful, rewarding career that uses your talents and the skills that you developed throughout your education. In this chapter, we are going to explore what this might mean and how you can pursue it. As you consider the many opportunities, we encourage you to consider the tone you are setting, both in your own thoughts and in how you present yourself to others, including your classmates and professors. The tone we recommend is that you are a highly skilled individual who has much to offer across a variety of sectors, and that the right opportunity is out there for you. Because, if you have been following our suggestions throughout the book, this should be true.

With that mindset in place, let's get started.

Do I need to choose between pursuing a "regular" career or an academic career?

Discussions of PhD careers have been slow to embrace reality. During the now-long-ago golden age of academic hiring, a misleading "PhD = academic job" equation solidified in the social sciences and humanities, ignoring the fact that PhDs have always ended up in a wide variety of career outcomes. After the academic hiring bubble burst, discussion of "non-academic alternatives for PhDs" emerged gradually, moving about as fast as an ocean liner turning around. And unfortunately, career discussions still tend to take an overwhelmingly bifurcated approach—academic versus "other" (with evolving terms such as Plan B, post-academic, alt-ac, and more). As we have stated from the start, we categorically reject this. We reject the implicit (or more often than not explicit) ranking that frames things in an academia-first mindset that privileges tenure-track positions as the primary goal, with everything else a consolation prize. This book has sought to guide you to maximize your PhD to realize your larger goal of a successful and rewarding career, period. Your PhD experience provides you with a wealth of training and knowledge that you can use as a springboard into a multitude of career opportunities.

We encourage you to retain academia as *an* option (we discuss academic jobs specifically in chapter 9 for this reason), but not as your only option, nor necessarily as your preferred option. One does not need to look far (often not far down the hallways of one's doctoral department) to find disaffected academics. Academia is a job with many positive aspects; we both feel it is a privileged position to hold and understand fully why so many people wish to secure an academic career. At the same time, like all jobs it is, well, a job, and it has its negative aspects. Some people realize they hate teaching or research. The ambiguity and lack of structure can be demoralizing for some faculty members. And since people rarely leave, some academic units go for decades with unhappy individuals trapped together in a toxic environment. Assuming that an academic position will necessarily result in career satisfaction is risky.

At the same time that we ask you to avoid an academia-first mentality, we also caution against academia-last thinking. Some PhDs decide there is no way they will pursue a traditional academic career, sometimes even before they start the degree or while in the midst of it, and focus entirely on other options. While this is healthier than academia-or-bust, we'll go the other way and defend academia as a job option even for people who can't wait to escape the ivory tower. It is possible there are academic opportunities that really suit you.

Thus, we encourage you to not rule anything out and to explore multiple options, simultaneously, and then pick from the best options available to you. We want to stress the word "simultaneously." Some students plan (and we use that word generously) a sequential approach, intending to pursue academic positions first to see if things pan out (the academia-first mentality in action). This is highly risky. The harsh reality is that you can do everything possible to set yourself up for academic career success—a peer-reviewed publication record that would earn you tenure; grant success; teaching experience at multiple levels along with strong student evaluations and a certificate from your university's teaching centre; a prestigious postdoc working with Dr. Bigshot at Topnotch University—and still end up without a tenure-track job offer. And, insult upon injury, academic job interviews can become harder to secure as time since the doctoral defence accumulates, since there can be prejudice among some academic hiring committees that "if they were any good, they'd have a job by now," ignoring the realities of the academic job market. The academia-first mentality results in far too many individuals making economically and emotionally damaging choices: decisions to take on years of contingent sessional teaching (see our discussion on the sessional trap below) or to act as an academic nomad, moving across the country from one short-term position to another, straining personal relationships and possibly a partner's career prospects, as they search for that increasingly elusive tenure-track Holy Grail. Bottom line: We strongly advise against pursuing academic positions exclusively. If you do decide to ignore other possibilities and only pursue opportunities within academia in the hope that a tenure-track position turns up, it is vital that you set a firm deadline (such as one to two years) after which you will aggressively broaden your career search. And tell everyone you know about your self-imposed deadline, so that they will hold you accountable to stick to it.

What is the "sessional trap"?

There is a well-documented phenomenon known as the *adjunct/sessional trap*, in which a newly minted PhD (or worse, a PhD student) finds occasional work teaching courses as a sessional instructor .. and keeps on teaching as a sessional, course by course and year after year as their primary source of income. (We should note that this is different from teaching an occasional course while holding a full-time position elsewhere.) While at first it appears to be a good opportunity—paid work, experience, joy of teaching— over time it can turn into the opposite. Teaching by piecework eats up enormous time and energy, and the low pay, lack of security, and general randomness of opportunities can mean a poor quality of life. It is difficult to keep focused on finishing your dissertation or advancing research and publishing, which are the determining factors in most academic hires. And yet, it is work that pays, it is related to one's PhD, and it requires no heavy lifting (other than exam booklets). It is difficult to walk away, and yet equally difficult to get ahead. While people in the sessional trap occasionally get academic jobs because of their great teaching experience, this is the exception rather than the norm. Let us state that more bluntly, in case you are tempted to gloss over it: The chances that years on the sessional teaching hamster wheel will result in a tenure-track position start at very low and diminish further over time. Hence the label "trap."

So, do you need to choose between pursuing a regular or an academic career? No. If your goal is a rewarding career, period, your strategy should be to find opportunities to grow and show that growth through accomplishment. Keeping academia as a viable option does require clear and ongoing links to the scholarly world, ideally by publishing and attending academic conferences, that keep you current and connected. But it does not require staying in a single "academic" groove of precarious employment through postdocs, term positions, and sessional gigs. If you are concerned that a hypothetical future academic search committee will penalize you for taking on more diversified opportunities, consider a strong counternarrative: Having career experience in other sectors enables you to bring real-world experience to research and the classroom. You set the tone, and you decide what to include on your CV.

Look for opportunities wherever they can be found. There is no Plan B. It's all Plan A.

What are my career options as a PhD?

One reason why academia ends up being the default option for so many PhDs is its simplicity and obviousness—it's right there. Other options and opportunities are spread out widely and thus can be confusing and overwhelming. Furthermore, while academic jobs inevitably ask for people with a PhD in a specific discipline, not many other positions say "must have PhD." It can be admittedly difficult to understand and identify what career opportunities are out there for you because, with some exceptions, they are rarely exclusive to PhDs.

As stated, jobs are solutions to problems, and employers are seeking individuals with the ability to address their problems. This means you need to wrap your mind around an important fact: With the exception of academia, hiring is typically based on competencies, not on credentials or academic disciplines. In most sectors, the PhD is rarely important by itself; rather, it's the competencies you developed in it that will get you the interview and possibly the job. Indeed, whether you actually finished your PhD may not be that important at all. And even if the employer values the completed degree, they usually don't care about the disciplinary label. They may value specific skills and knowledge bases that are typically found in specific disciplines, but an employer seeking someone with qualitative research skills (as an example) may not care whether or not the individual comes from a sociology, history, or other disciplinary background.

There are numerous sectors in which you can solve others' problems, and the universe of options that can fit your goal of a successful, rewarding career that uses your talents and skills is constantly expanding (see Figure 8.1 and Table 8.1 showing some common PhD career paths for some initial ideas). Build off these ideas through your own research. In particular, look into your disciplinary association's resources for PhD career options in your field, and the more generalized information available in higher education media outlets, books, and websites devoted entirely to non-academic careers for PhDs. As you explore, the most ubiquitous information you will likely find are profiles and personal narratives of individuals and their post-PhD careers. While sometimes short on practical advice, especially the more eclectic their career paths, these can be inspiring. Immerse yourself in as many of

FIGURE 8.1: Universe of careers for PhDs

TABLE 8.1 Selected examples of careers in which PhDs thrive

	WHY	PROS	CONS
Corporate Consulting	Entire, often very elite, companies are dedicated to analyzing and solving business problems. They want highly educated, analytical people. Like you.	Get to work all day on complex problems and how to solve them—and get paid well to do it.	Often involves travel, long hours, and high pressure. While PhDs are valued, MBAs are usually valued more.
Market Research	Many firms are started by PhDs and are always interested in people with strong research skills—both quantitative and qualitative.	Sometimes interesting work; sometimes good money.	Must have actual specific skills. Possible lifetime of guiding focus groups and designing surveys about topics that don't interest you.
Not-for-Profit Sector (including think tanks)	Organizations dedicated to solving problems, doing good, and generally saving the world. May be an attractive fit for the idealism and dedication of some PhDs.	Often meaningful and interesting work, just like grad school.	Often lower pay and lack of job security, just like grad school.
Tenure-Track Academia	See "default" above.	Good pay; exceptional job security once tenure is achieved. Mandatory variety: you teach, research, and do administrative service.	Perhaps you don't enjoy the idea of having to always teach, always research, and always do administrative service. Same co-workers for decades. University may be located in a city that you prefer not to live in, trapping you there until retirement.
University Administrative Careers	Universities are large, complicated places that need intelligent people to keep them running. And they tend to value educational credentials.	Get to stay in the university environment; possible continuing opportunities to teach or research.	Anomie and cognitive dissonance as you are constantly reminded that you are a PhD, but not faculty.

(Continued)

TABLE 8.1 Selected examples of careers in which PhDs thrive (Continued)

	WHY	PROS	CONS
Public/ Corporate Affairs	Refers to the parts of large companies dedicated to public, media, and government relations, and internal corporate information and processes. Tends to attract smart, analytical people with good writing and communication skills—such as PhDs.	Good money; sometimes interesting work; great holiday parties.	Fuzzy job security as these areas are usually first in line for downsizing; risk of spending your time writing soul-destroying bland press releases; possibility of working for Dr. Evil (who also has a doctorate).
Government	Public services look for smart people with high levels of education to help run the country/ province/municipality.	Decent pay, reasonable job security; prospects of variety and advancement.	Slow and complex hiring; possibly excessive concern with protocol and process (we're looking at you, federal government); incremental work (see more on government jobs below).
Politics	Myriad jobs within local, provincial, and national political party organizations and legislative and ministerial offices. Research and communication skills developed in PhD programs can be put to immediate application.	Power; excitement; people take your calls.	Partisanship and blind team loyalty are required. Long hours; sometimes middling pay; no job security. Can take over your life. And the day after an electoral defeat, no one picks up when you call.
Publishing and Communications	A wide field that includes online and print publications, professional writing, editing, marketing, and more. Good writing, text, and presentation skills are important.	Working with words, and other people who are also interested in words, is, in a single word, awesome. In ideal cases, your life is dedicated to books. Books! Books!	Volatile industry subject to technological change; high reliance on part-time and contractual employment; tolerance for poor grammar is non-existent.
Sales	Higher-end products and services depend heavily on informed salespeople who actually understand the complex things they are selling. An often overlooked career opportunity for PhDs.	Interaction with people; the satisfaction of succeeding; a highly transferable skill you can take to different employers and contexts.	Possibly volatile income and unpredictable routines and hours; may involve considerable travel.
Arts and Cultural Institutions	Museums, galleries, and other arts organizations draw heavily on highly educated people who can apply their knowledge and competencies.	Can apply direct knowledge from many disciplines; work on the same things you did in your PhD.	Likely a crowded job market; pay and job security vary widely; possible conflicts between artistic/ intellectual values and the priorities of the organization.

these profiles as possible, and look for parallels and ideas that you can emulate in your own career search. You may also find statistics on what sectors and industries people like you end up in, or other systematic data relevant to you, your discipline, and your own experience. While it will vary, the data may give you some ideas on possible options and their likelihood of success.

Your PhD program and the experiences you developed alongside it provided you with skills and knowledge that make you an asset to many possible people and organizations. But having competencies and knowledge relevant to a career and enjoying that particular career are not the same thing. While you are qualified to do a range of things, what will make you happy may be a bit more narrow.

Earlier, we recommended that you simultaneously pursue a few options that might be a good fit. So start by identifying three or four that appeal to you. More information will help you to identify these, and in chapter 4 we recommended that you build information by deliberately engaging in activities beyond your program (such as taking career development classes, conducting informational interviews, and volunteering). If you have done so, you likely have a number of ideas for careers that might fit your particular interests and profile; if you have not, it is time to do so, and as informational interviews are particularly valuable in this regard, we suggest you lean into these heavily. But in addition to gathering information, you must do a bit of self-reflection. For some people, this is a bumpy road, so buckle up.

Do PhDs go out on their own?

Accustomed to the large and comforting arms of universities, most PhDs (and most people generally) envision working in an organization, whether big or small, public or private. But some create their own jobs and businesses, and this may be an option for you. This may involve working as an independent contractor or consultant (by choice, rather than as a foot in the door to a permanent job), starting an enterprise that produces goods or services, and other options that ideally make use of the skills you developed in your PhD to solve a problem or need that you have identified. Unfortunately, entrepreneurship is rarely presented as an option for PhDs, and it calls on a range of additional skills such as budgeting, marketing, and sales that are unlikely to be taught or cultivated in social science and humanities doctoral programs. The good news is that you may have access to such training on your campus and be able to tap into courses, alumni networks, and other resources (especially informational interviews) that can help you identify and then build the skills you need to go out on your own; such skills are often valued by employers and organizations as well. Bottom line: Make sure you consider self-employment as a strong option alongside others.

How do I figure out what I want to do?

The "what do you want to be when you grow up" question is intimidating, whether one is 6 ("explorer!") or 46 ("big data analyst!"... still a type of explorer). So much of our identities are wrapped up in career labels, and if you feel a small surge of panic at this question you are not alone. Note that the question is not "what *can* I do" (you can do lots of things) but "what do I *want* to do." To help guide you to some answers to this question, we present three dimensions—activities, subject matter, and work environment—each with their own series of questions.

Activities

What energizes you? What are you doing—what exact kind of work are you doing—when you lose track of time? What tasks do you find you want to go back to when you are interrupted? What is the common element? Psychologist Mihaly Csikszentmihalyi is identified with the concept of a state of flow: a feeling of being fully immersed and satisfyingly absorbed in a task that is challenging and rewarding. So what triggers your flow? What consistently gives you the right balance of being challenged but not overwhelmed? What you are looking for is an overlap between your dominant competencies and the types of work that energize you. Consider the common activities that PhDs engage in, and identify which ones jazz you up and which ones wear you out, along with evidence and examples. (Also ask others for their observations of what makes you flow. Some things may be so natural to you that you don't realize they are exceptional.)

TABLE 8.2 Worksheet: Self-assessment of activities

COMMON CAREER-RELEVANT PHD ACTIVITIES	HOW I FEEL WHEN DOING ACTIVITY (ENERGIZED? DEPLETED? BORED? EXCITED? STRESSED? MIXED? OTHER?)	EVIDENCE/EXAMPLES OF FLOW
Reading and absorbing text: Humanities and most social science PhD students typically spend a lot of time reading, interpreting, and absorbing the written word. As most people in the world prefer watching videos to reading long texts, this is a definite strength and skill that PhDs bring to a range of professional opportunities.		
Gathering information: Many PhD students gather, organize, and preserve data (qualitative or quantitative) and understand the power of information, not only to analyze specific phenomena, but also to provide context, perspective, and institutional memory. Technological change means it is constantly easier to collect and analyze information, and this compulsion for data drives many modern organizations.		
Analyzing phenomena: Analysis is the heart of academic work and underlies nearly all dissertations. This can take many forms: breaking things down, separating and classifying their parts, and looking for patterns, connections, and relationships, all in a methodical, structured, and replicable manner. This is a valuable skill that is much rarer than most PhD students realize, because it is second nature to them and their academic peers.		
Structured interaction with people: Your PhD program likely involved a lot of structured interactions with people, through TAing/teaching, seminar discussions, and perhaps research interviews and other areas where there were some structured norms and boundaries to guide the discussion. Successfully completing these activities involved listening to people, drawing them out, and synthesizing perspectives—all activities that are practised in many careers.		

(Continued)

TABLE 8.2 Worksheet: Self-assessment of activities (Continued)

COMMON CAREER-RELEVANT PHD ACTIVITIES	HOW I FEEL WHEN DOING ACTIVITY (ENERGIZED? DEPLETED? BORED? EXCITED? STRESSED? MIXED? OTHER?)	EVIDENCE/EXAMPLES OF FLOW
Mentoring others: Many PhDs find they have a natural affinity toward helping and guiding others, be they undergraduate students in their tutorials or classes, more recent PhD students, or others. This skill is valuable in many management careers, where motivating and guiding others to success is key.		
Writing: PhD programs typically involve a lot of writing, and this *may* also mean that you can write in a clear and engaging manner. To be frank, this is something that *some* PhDs are good at, but not as much as we would like, as the kind of writing prized by academics and dissertation committees (i.e., the bigger the words and longer the sentences, the better) is not prized in the rest of the world. But if you find your words flow well, that you enjoy writing for different audiences, and if other people (ideally people from non-academic realms) mention that you write well, then that is a real asset. Because most people can't do that.		
Public speaking: A significant part of a PhD program involves public performance, whether it's class presentations, presenting seminar and conference papers, lecturing, or leading discussion groups, not to mention the performance that is your dissertation defence. Speaking to others and presenting complex information, verbally communicating information and ideas to audiences, and effectively managing non-verbal elements such as timing, positioning, and presentation of visual information (including tables and charts) is intimidating to many people and a valuable skill for those who excel at it.		
Project management: As we have said numerous times already, many of the accomplishments achieved by PhDs require and demonstrate project management skills; examples include publications, teaching, and (perhaps obviously) the dissertation itself. The ability to manage multiple-staged tasks successfully is an asset in all sectors.		

Build off of this list to think about the things in life that oddly capture your enthusiasm. Perhaps you keep a database of the weather patterns for your daily commute. You may have calculated down to exact measurements and number of steps the most efficient routes to every building on campus, or gone into stores offering to rewrite all their signs and promotions because the writing is so poor. Can you identify moments or incidents that really engaged you? Has there been a particular small project, a meeting or event, an article, or a person that has made you think, "Wow, that's really interesting," even if the next thought was, "but I'd better get back to my disser-tation"? Now is the time to reflect again on those quick moments of inspiration. What exactly was it that captivated you? These types of things are further data points to help you identify what moti-vates and absorbs you.

Subject matter

Consider the topics that grab your attention, both in your PhD work, in your real-life activities, and in the things you read, shows you watch, and news you follow. Removing yourself from the idea of careers, jobs, and employment, what is the range of topics that you feel a pull toward? What *topics* inspire your curiosity? We suggested you avoid the word "passion" when deciding whether or not to do a PhD, but we will allow it here: What *things* are you passionate about? Child poverty? The environment? Urban transit? What hurts your heart? What angers you? What inspires you? Just as we said above that hiring is not about filling a job, but rather about solving a problem, think now about problems, issues, or areas you feel strongly about and where you dream of making a contribution—even if you can't think of a specific job that matches up.

Our experience: Jonathan

One of my odder career breakthroughs during my PhD was reading a business article on a company that made office furniture. It talked a lot about trends in offices: open concept, cubicles, and early experiments in "desk-free" environments. I wasn't that interested in the business of selling chairs, but I was fascinated by the questions of how people work and interact and the effect of different setups on organizational culture and productivity. This tied into my public administration dissertation and accelerated my interest in how organizations and the people within them work, and it gave me a lot of ideas about career options outside of academia. And while I ended up in academia anyway, this also fuelled my early entry into administrative roles as a faculty member. I've never forgotten that article.

Environment

What sort of environment do you want to work in? A large or small organization? Part of a large team or mostly by yourself? How do you feel about going out on your own and being self-employed or head of an enterprise? Do you crave a dynamic daily (or hourly or minute-by-minute) environment, or a slower pace? This may feel challenging since you likely have limited personal experience to draw on, and picturing yourself in alternative scenarios can be difficult. There is also an understandable temptation to prioritize things you don't currently have, such as the financial and job security more typically found in large organizations. But think of this less in terms of a hypothetical dream job and more as the workplace characteristics that attract and energize you. Stability or change? Organization and structure or (controlled) chaos? Everyone is different; there's no right or wrong answers here, and they do not necessarily match up with a particular type of organization or workplace. But there will be things that make you feel more energized and excited, and others that will not. Some of these revolve around people and relationships. You may be energized by the idea of working with a variety of people in a flat and fluid reporting structure, or you may value a more predictable hierarchical environment where roles and relations are fixed and clear. Consider also tasks and purposes. Do you like the idea of having specific things to do, or are you comfortable with figuring out your role(s) as you go along? Are you drawn to a team that exists around a fixed project and then reorganizes or dissolves, or a permanent operation that carries out ongoing tasks? And also think about routines. Typically as people grow older or develop family responsibilities they are more drawn to fixed or self-directed flexible hours and not as happy about unpredictable hours or coming in on the weekend as needed, but it's still useful to picture which appeals to you. You can also think about office layouts; for example, are you energized or horrified by working in an office without assigned desks where everyone just grabs a spot as needed? Again, we're not building your hypothetical perfect job here, we are exploring the workplace values and characteristics that attract you.

Should I seek a government job?

Canada's public sector—including federal, provincial, and municipal governments, not to mention quasi-government bodies—has numerous career options of interest for PhDs. However, while PhDs are valued in theory (and may lead to an automatic pay increase just for possessing the credential) and there can even be special recruitment programs for them, the fit is not always automatic. A key tension is that what academics consider to be empirical, applied work can still come off as too scholarly and theoretical to public servants. Governments value the skills and competencies developed in the PhD—but like other employers they rarely want to hear about your dissertation.

Government covers a vast range of work, and while some areas can be dynamic and rewarding, it has a well-deserved reputation for being slow, hierarchical, and risk averse—particularly the larger the organization and the more complex the issues. Irony and a healthy sense of the absurd is sometimes needed to roll with the punches and put up with yet another interdepartmental meeting to discuss the ninth draft of a proposal before the deputy minister or director changes their mind. If you keep that in mind, many people like the variety and interest they find in government work and really do feel they are making a difference and serving the public. And while job security is not as guaranteed as it is in academia, it is usually strong with comparable pay and benefits.

Determining your priorities

Once you have determined the activities you like to do, the topics you like to engage with, and the type of workplace environment you prefer, you must give some thought to what matters the most to you. You can then use this self-knowledge to think in multiple directions to identify those three or four career options (academia may be one of them) that might be a good fit for you. Let's say that your priority is to engage in the activities of analyzing phenomena and writing, preferably but not necessarily working independently or in a small team, and that subject matter is of less concern to you. This might suggest that analyst positions in business, government, or the not-for-profit sector are a good fit. Let's say your priority is to draw upon your disciplinary knowledge, ideally but not necessarily through public speaking and structured interactions with people, and work environment is the least important factor to you. If so, perhaps a government or public relations position drawing on your disciplinary background is an option to consider. You get the idea. Push yourself to break apart the components. What would a government or publishing career that uses your deep understanding of history, sociology, or gender studies look like? Are there university jobs beyond the traditional academic track that require information gathering skills?

Answering these questions requires active engagement. As you narrow in on ideas, aim to do additional rounds of informational interviews, both to gather information and to build your networks. Research industries and sectors. And listen to your gut: As you move closer toward an idea, do you find yourself growing warmer to it, or does your enthusiasm cool off? This process takes time and many iterations and is best approached as a research challenge. Every option you find that does work for you, and every option you find that does not, are simply more data points. At some point, some clear career options should emerge, and you can start looking for and pursuing opportunities.

Should I hire a professional career consultant or coach?

Some professional career coaches and consultants specialize in working one on one with PhD graduates (as well as individuals who have chosen to discontinue their PhD programs) on career development matters. Many of these consultants have PhDs themselves and thus have a detailed and sympathetic understanding of academic training and culture. Some function as a coach, helping PhDs think carefully through career options, personal aptitudes, and possible career paths, while others provide more narrow assistance such as working directly with PhDs to create application materials (cover letters, résumés) and conduct job searches. For many PhDs, these personalized services can be invaluable: Working individually with a professional career consultant provides a form of accountability and structure that can be motivating, and the individualized questions and personal feedback can help to prompt thoughtful action. If you do aim to make the investment, do the necessary background research to ensure the individual has the track record that you need and an approach that fits your own style, and understand that the consultant's primary role is to help direct you and keep you accountable to your goals: You still need to do the work.

Once I have an idea of what I want to do, how do I get started?

Employment opportunities can occur formally, through advertised competitions (academic positions fall into this camp), or informally, through personal networks and what sometimes feels like random chance. What is important to understand is that there is no PhD-specific way to look for jobs; you have to follow the same job search strategies that individuals without PhDs (including those without any degree or credential at all) follow. What you do have on your side are (1) finely tuned research skills, (2) access to university or graduate faculty career services (as they share your interest in seeing you employed), and (3) access to departmental alumni and other networks. Furthermore, there are online career opportunity information sites for PhDs generally, and in some cases in specific disciplines. As you begin your search, a good starting point can be a meeting with your university's career counselling services. The helpfulness of these units varies, but you may be pleasantly surprised.

The larger and more professional the organization, the more likely it is that it has formal advertisement and application processes for its permanent positions. Governments can have particularly formal and sometimes very slow hiring practices, but they do run recruitment programs that call for general applications; while some are tied to specialized skills, others explicitly target PhDs and similar advanced degrees. Private and for-profit companies are less likely to hold general recruitment competitions that specifically target social science and humanities disciplines (their loss), but don't assume that competitions that seem focused on STEM and business graduates are off limits to you. Ensure you know—by talking to career centres and doing your own research—when those competitions take place and which ones might be appropriate for you. You should also look carefully for co-op and summer positions, in government and elsewhere, through university career centres. While usually directed at undergraduates and possibly not a great use of your total PhD education, some are more advanced and your graduate status may give you an edge at building up valuable experience and connections.

There is a widespread truism that "90 per cent [or 80 per cent, 70 per cent, whatever] of jobs are not advertised." This is particularly true for temporary, part-time, and contractual labour (which can serve as an important foot in the door for future opportunities, including in government), and for smaller organizations and operations where the boss is also the entire human resources department. In those contexts, connections, references, and word of mouth may be the primary entry point, especially when speedily filling the job is a priority. The networks and professional reputation you have built (see chapters 4 and 7) can be vital in opening up job opportunities. You may learn about an opportunity because X mentions to Y they have a problem and need someone to solve it, and Y immediately thinks of you and passes on your name.

Should I get professional qualifications?

There can be advantages to getting professional qualifications, such as certificates in project management, financial management, coaching, and so forth. Lifelong learning is always a good thing, and pursuing professional certificates can advance (and provide evidence of) your knowledge and competencies. Further, professional training is often applied in nature, and thus useful in helping you see how you might contribute positively to a variety of workplaces. As these programs can be expensive and time consuming, ask yourself whether the designation is necessary for the career opportunity. If so, consider starting a professional designation, listing this as "in process" on your résumé, and pursue it while (rather than instead of) pursuing job opportunities.

How I can make my application materials more competitive?

Recall our key theme: Jobs typically materialize to solve one or more problems. Your competencies, your abilities, your "flow" may be the solution to that problem (and are certainly the solution to *somebody's* problem). But employers, be it an academic search committee, a human resources department, or a single person, sort through dozens or hundreds of applications for the typical professional position. In large competitions, applications may be automatically scanned and sorted by software before even reaching a human being, though this is less likely the more specialized and professional the position. While one would like to think that each application gets equal scrutiny, time restraints generally do not permit employers to search for hidden diamonds in the rough. Some great prospects are overlooked because the applicant does not accurately present their strengths (or alternatively, inaccurately presents their strengths, leading to crushing disappointment all around at the interview stage). It is up to you as the applicant to make a case for yourself—a strong case for yourself—that you are not only a strong candidate for *a* position, but more specifically that you are a strong candidate for *this exact* position. The employer is looking for the ideal candidate to solve their problem, and you are well served to help make that connection for them.

Social science and humanities PhDs are often trained to understand the importance of language, narrative, and framing. They are also typically trained to understand the importance of seeing things from different perspectives. These ingrained understandings will benefit you as you consider how your many experiences and competencies can be expressed in ways that make sense to potential employers. Thinking about framing and narrative is critical because, again, hiring is about *solving the employer's problem* and you want to ensure that, as much as possible, your application presents you as the solution to their problem.

Of course, you may not actually know what their exact problem is. But you can conduct some basic research that will help. The first stop is obviously the job ad or description itself. Your second stop is the organizational website. To the extent that information is publicly available, get a sense of the organizational structure and where the unit to which you are applying fits. Is there a strategic plan or other similar types of documentation available? Overall, based on the information that you can find from the website, how do you think the unit sees itself and its future, and how does this tie to the larger organizational mission? Now there is an excellent chance that the individuals directly involved in the hiring for this specific position have never read their organization's strategic plan, or may not even know there is a strategic plan. But it is possible that they have read it, and the reason they are able to hire for a vacant position is because someone convinced somebody else that the position solves a problem that must be addressed as part of the strategic plan. Your application will be seen and filtered through many eyes, some of whom value the goals and visions of the larger institution. For your final set of clues about the problem to be solved, conduct basic research on the sector and organization more broadly. Has the organization been in the news for any reason, positive or negative? Have there been economic or demographic trends that are affecting the sector in general?

Armed with all of this information, you can make an educated guess about the problem that the organization is seeking to solve through hiring, and you are now ready to start preparing your application materials that make the case you are not just a worthy candidate for the position, but the solution—the best solution—to this problem. Most job applications will require that you submit a cover letter and either a résumé or CV; academic jobs almost always require additional material that we address specifically in chapter 9. Some positions, particularly for large organizations, may require applying through a standardized portal that imposes word limits or other constraints; be sure to follow the rules yet do whatever you can to personalize things within the requirements. What is important to remember is that your application materials have exactly one objective, and that is to get you an in-person interview. Not the job—the interview.

Your cover letter is critical; this is usually where employers will start (and in some cases end) their review of applications for professional positions. Instead of thinking of this letter as an introduction, think of it as a sales document, with you selling the idea that you are a candidate worthy of one of the few interview spots. In sales, you have to keep the buyer in mind; in this case, you need to think carefully about what *this particular* employer needs to seriously consider your application. Here is where you can draw heavily on your background research.

Aim to be specific, direct, and evidence based. If the position description mentions a particular theme, and you legitimately have background in the area, state your evidence of this clearly in your letter. If the job ad states they are looking for someone who can do Q, R, S, and T, explicitly provide the evidence of why you are qualified to do Q and T.

You want to make sure that your cover letter fits with the position itself. Many applications that employers receive show all the signs of a "cut and paste" effort, in which the applicant just replaced the organizational name in the cover letter. We recognize that it is tough to personalize things when you are applying over and over to different positions, but make at least some effort to avoid the above. When job searches are a buyer's market, you as the seller must take steps to position yourself uniquely for the particular job. Use the cover letter as an opportunity to demonstrate you have in fact done your research on the organization. And before you submit the application, proofread carefully. Be sure to spell the institution's name correctly (no one is hiring at "Carlton University" [proper name: Carleton] or the "University of Saskatoon" [proper name: University of Saskatchewan]), and it is not impressive when you tell a federal department how much you want to work for the Government of British Columbia. If you mention specific people by name that you look forward to working with, make sure that (1) they are in fact a member of the exact unit you are applying to and (2) you spell their name correctly. Finally, watch out for vague or misleading information. Don't say you have a PhD and then add in smaller print "all but dissertation." Don't try to pass off teaching assistant work as independently teaching a class. Be specific and provide evidence. If the employer thinks you are trying to fudge details, it leaves a bad taste no matter how strong the rest of your application is.

Your university undoubtedly offers a host of services for résumé and CV preparation, and these services are often available to alumni as well as current students. The important thing to note is that you want to tailor the résumé or CV to the specific job application. Most people are aware of the need for this for résumés; as résumés only have a few pages of space, the importance of strategically using this space to create a case that you are the solution to the employer's problem is pretty obvious. But even CVs should be approached in a strategic manner with different ordering and presentation of information depending on the position.

Who should I list as references?

Just as you are tailoring your application materials to the position, you want to be strategic in how you select your job references. For career opportunities outside of academia, you likely want to have references who can speak to your work habits and aptitudes in addition to your academic references, and here is where some of your non-program pursuits can really pay off. Even for academic career opportunities, you should think strategically about the job and your references: Applications for research-focused positions (including most tenure-track positions) are strengthened by references that speak to your research excellence and potential, whereas applications for teaching-focused positions will ideally include references who can speak to your teaching ability. The larger principle to keep returning to is that you are actively seeking to meet *their* needs, and you want to think carefully about all elements of your application to ensure that there is a consistent and compelling message that you are the ideal solution to their problem. At the same time, be careful not to inadvertently raise red flags: If your references exclude your current employer or your dissertation supervisor, it may raise questions. Again, look carefully at all materials through the eyes of your audience.

How can I get strong references?
There are two parts to getting the reference you want: (1) asking people to be a reference, and (2) giving them the information they need to be a good reference; sometimes

this second point is forgotten or not handled well. The first part requires some frankness with potential referees, and there is no substitute for explicitly asking, "Can you give me a *strong* reference?" Not asking that direct question traps referees with only a modest view of your abilities into a corner, and most shy away from frankness themselves and instead scribble or mumble a tepid reference that does little for you. But second, make sure to give referees as much (carefully organized and presented) information as possible to ensure they can tailor their reference to your full, up-to-date strengths and the specific requirements of the opportunity. Many enthusiastic references miss the mark as they stumble through a phone call not prepared to describe your skills that relate to the job at hand, or write three pages praising your research prowess for a teaching position. It is in your interest to make the effort to provide your referee with the information necessary to help you achieve your goal.

How do I prepare for an interview?

Your application materials get you the interview, and it is at the interview itself that the real sales work is done. Once you have an interview lined up, your preparation work should move into high gear. You will want to know how long the interview will last and have a sense of whom exactly you will be meeting with; it is reasonable for you to ask these questions in advance. Furthermore, keep in mind that even though the employer has a problem they need to solve, your particular interview is more important to you than to them. You may be the fourth person they are interviewing for the position, or they may be preoccupied with other matters.

To prepare, you want to (1) identify for yourself what information you want to be certain they have about you by the time you leave the room and (2) anticipate what questions you are likely to encounter. Your goal is to be proactive and to have an agenda for yourself, rather than just reacting to their questions. What is your sales pitch, your case for yourself as the solution to their problem? Having this sorted out in your own head prior to the interview is critical.

Start by identifying three to five key competencies that you bring to the position, tying these to words and phrases that they use themselves in the job posting. Then, link these competencies to specific evidence and experience. Aim to use a narrative, real-life example to provide evidence of your ability in an area. For example, if your goal is to demonstrate that you have financial and budgeting skills, you could tell the story of how you served as the Graduate Student Association's financial officer and talk about your specific accomplishments in that position.

Identify a number of similar narrative stories (ideally five or more), making sure you are specific about what you *individually* did, how your actions were tied to your own personal agency and skills, and how the activity had results. Ensure that your stories are rich with detail, even while you keep them brief: "Last April I was the lead organizer for a teaching panel at my discipline's national conference" is more compelling than "I once organized a panel at a conference." As you identify these narratives, you can start to see how they can be adapted to the types of interview questions that tend to occur in job interviews, be they in academia, the private sector, government, or any other field. Often, interviewers ask applicants to "Tell us about a time that you failed" or "What was your role in [project/paper listed in application materials]?" By having narrative stories planned in advance, you can ensure that your answers to the questions are not simply reactive responses, but rather are strategic efforts to continue to sell yourself as the solution to their problem.

With your interview goals in hand ("I want to demonstrate that I have skills A, B, and C") and your bank of evidence clarified ("I will tell them about experiences Q, R, S, and T"), you then need to practise. Prepare written bullet point responses for as many obvious questions as possible (see the worksheet in Table 8.3, and ask your supervisor, graduate chair, and other students for more ideas). These written responses should be short and full of concrete examples and evidence rather than vague platitudes. After you have done this, ask your graduate program to assist you in setting up a practice interview, either based on your prepared list or (better still) on a list of questions they come up with themselves. Write down their questions and then repeat the process with a group of peers. As you practise, get comfortable with rephrasing questions back if the wording or intent

TABLE 8.3 Worksheet: Interview questions you must be prepared for

QUESTION	TIPS AND CONSIDERATIONS	YOUR RESPONSE
What interests you about this position? Why do you want to work here? Where does this opportunity fit in your long-term career plan?	Address both the specific job and the larger context/environment.	
What do you know about our organization?	Demonstrate your preparation with key publicly available facts about the organization and its priorities. Paraphrase rather than just repeat information to show you understand what it means and have not just memorized it.	
Tell us about a time when you: demonstrated leadership; led a project; failed; solved a problem; managed conflict; dealt with a tight deadline; worked with a diverse group of people.	Tell a narrative, but not a longwinded story with all the details. Present all aspects positively or as benignly as possible; no one wants a complainer or a gossip.	
This seems like a change in direction for you. Why are you interested in this position?	Articulate a broader picture of your career trajectory and goals that avoids suggesting this is a temporary detour.	
What would make you a good colleague/analyst/employee?	This is not about how you are a friendly person who gets along with everyone, but the value you would bring to the team and organization.	

(Continued)

TABLE 8.3 Worksheet: Interview questions you must be prepared for (Continued)

QUESTION	TIPS AND CONSIDERATIONS	YOUR RESPONSE
How do you deal with diversity in the workplace?	This type of question is typically answered in a vague manner. Be prepared to impress them by having a specific example of how you have managed diverse tutorial sessions or other similar situations.	
What is your ideal work environment? What work environments would you find challenging?	Describe your preferences in terms of what stimulates and motivates you to do your best. Answer truthfully, or you might end up getting hired into your definition of hell.	
Why should we hire you?	This is not about your qualifications, but how you will solve their problem.	
Do you have any questions for us?	You should have a written list on hand. Questions should focus on organizational goals and objectives more than the specific job.	

is unclear, and pay attention to whether your answers are short and on point or rambling and unfocused. Keep practising.

Be extremely conscious of the tone you are setting. For non-academic positions, you want to ensure you avoid two pitfalls common to PhDs on the job market. The first is creating the sense that the job you are applying for is not the job you actually want. If you position yourself as ready to jump ship as soon as an academic job opens up, you are positioning yourself as a bad risk for them. No one wants to be the second choice that will be abandoned at once if your desired employment suitor casts a glance in your direction. Since they may assume this, you want to be sure to convey sincere and lasting enthusiasm for the position. The second is creating the impression that you think you are overqualified for the position. Be careful about walking in with any sense that the position is somehow beneath you. Show excitement about the possibilities and all that you can bring to the position. Be someone you would want to hire.

What do I do after the interview?

Immediately after the interview, send an email to the lead person you met with thanking them for the opportunity to interview for the position and restating your interest in the position (assuming you are, in fact, still interested). If applicable, you should also send an email to the key staff person who arranged any logistic details, thanking them for their efforts. (The importance of being gracious to staff at all stages of the process cannot be overstated.) And then, after that, you wait. And wait. You do not contact them, or the staff, to inquire (nag) about your application. They are going as quickly as their institutional environment allows.

I found a great non-academic career. Should I try to keep one foot in the academic door?

We say again: There is only Plan A, and you should pursue a variety of career options from the start. But careers evolve, and people often move from one sector to another, so this raises the question of how much effort one should devote to keeping academia as an ongoing career option as other opportunities develop. As we say in the next chapter, academic hiring decisions revolve heavily around projecting a candidate's long-term future trajectory, and a lack of recent and current research activity (i.e., scholarly publications) gives search committees concern and makes it harder for them to see a promising trajectory. The PhD never expires, but to gain entry to an academic job interview, it needs to be supported by other accomplishments over time, demonstrating ongoing professional momentum.

Should you bother trying to maintain this momentum? Keeping up ties to stay immediately competitive for a tenure-track job becomes increasingly difficult as time goes on and you pursue other opportunities, since you may feel stretched in two directions, along with family and other life responsibilities. If you have a full-time job, staying up late to write academic articles and using your vacation time and stressed-out credit card to present at academic conferences, all to keep up your CV in case a tenure-track job comes along, becomes increasingly hard—possibly doable, but stressful and hard. Some people may not even notice the stress at first, because the academic world feels so familiar and comfortable. But in many cases they are slowly worn down as they try to straddle two different worlds.

Another option is just keeping up ties to see what might happen. This may include publishing or attending conferences, reading new scholarly publications that interest you, attending local university seminars and events, teaching sessionally, or anything else that energizes you and does not disrupt or distract from other career opportunities and life in general. Ideally some of these will connect with your full-time career, though this will vary, and they may ultimately just be more of a personal passion unconnected to your career. (Some people really do read scholarly journals just for fun … or so we understand.)

Our position is that you should invest your time and energy in things that give you the most career return on investment, or at least a high degree of personal satisfaction. Keeping one foot in the academic door may or may not be your best decision, depending on which of the two above forms it takes.

Our experience: Loleen

My return to academic life after a decade working outside academia is highly atypical, and it was also not planned. When I began my career I made no efforts to stay part of the academic world. I taught a sessional course when asked by my doctoral department because it needed an instructor for a particular course, not out of a desire to stay in the field. I attended the occasional academic conference when it was a good opportunity to present a particular research study. But I saw myself as having moved outside academic life and felt no particular angst about this; my PhD was being put to good use elsewhere, and I was truly enjoying my work. I ended up on the radar of my current department when I presented research at a combined academic–practitioner conference. A few years later a faculty member contacted me directly and asked me to apply for a position they were advertising. I was not watching academic job postings and would not have seen the posting on my own. The decision to apply was a difficult one for me; indeed, after accepting the position, I delayed my start date by a full year to continue to ponder my choice to leave think-tank life. The extent to which I kept a foot in the academic door was entirely directed by my interests at the time, and I never sought to walk back through.

So, how do I launch my career?

We started this chapter with reference to the business self-help classic *How to Win Friends and Influence People*. It is useful, we think, to look separately at the two parts of that title. First we have "win friends." The world is composed of small and interwoven networks. While search processes are normally confidential, in all aspects of the search (from your letter to your conduct at a job interview, should you get one) you are creating an impression, expanding your network, and building your professional reputation. Second is "influence people." How you present yourself can influence employers (people) to keep reading your application, to consider adding your name to a long list of possible candidates, to consider advocating that your name be included on a short list, and to contemplate championing you as the candidate to hire. At the same time, influence can only go so far; there are often larger dynamics at play (internal negotiations about the future direction of the organization, for example) that you cannot foresee.

Launching your career requires you to keep moving forward, keep exploring, and keep expanding your horizons. Your goal of a successful, rewarding career that uses your talents and the skills that you developed throughout your education is attainable. It may take some time to achieve, but we believe that a satisfying outcome awaits you.

You set the tone. Have we mentioned that already? You set the tone. We suggest you set the tone to optimism and possibility.

CHAPTER 9

APPROACH ACADEMIC JOBS STRATEGICALLY

At times it can seem that academic job markets function like lotteries: Buy a ticket and hope you somehow beat the odds. While the academic job market fluctuates, in most years and in most fields of the social sciences and humanities the supply of possible candidates vastly outstrips the number of available positions. A typical tenure-track job in Canada will receive dozens or even hundreds of applications. While it is easy to be discouraged, throughout this book we have encouraged you to keep academic jobs among the many possibilities open to you. In this chapter, we explore how you can be strategic in approaching academic job opportunities, applying last chapter's basic principle of positioning oneself as a solution to an organization's problem to the specific case of the academic job market. In doing so, we want to change your perspective from "How can I beat the odds and win the tenure-track jackpot prize?" to "How can I be the solution to a department's hiring problem?" Just like any other entity, academic units hire faculty to solve a problem. Having been part of numerous academic hiring searches over the years, we can say that understanding this basic idea is fundamental to positioning yourself as strongly as possible.

How do you present yourself as the solution to a department's hiring problem? Throughout this book we have kept returning to our guiding question: Given both my future goals and the information currently available to me, what is my best decision right now? Your future goal is clear—you want the interview, and probably the job—while obtaining the information available will take some research on your part. You need to do whatever work you can to assess the hiring department's needs. Research is your thing, after all.

What are the different types of academic jobs?

It is important to know the difference between various types of academic appointments, and terminology is inconsistent. While "tenure-track" or "tenure-stream" clearly means a position that is intended to be permanent if the person passes tenure review after a few years, positions with a fixed term, typically one to three years, may be called "term," "contractually limited," "visiting," or something else. Term appointments often carry a higher teaching load and may be at the rank of "instructor" or "lecturer" (usually at a lower rate of pay) instead of "assistant professor" to signify this. While tenure-track teaching-intensive instructor positions also exist, most tenure-track appointments are made at the assistant professor level to signify strong expectations for both teaching and research. Finally, "sessional," "contract," or "adjunct" instructors are typically hired for single classes. These phrasings are often thrown around imprecisely, so be alert.

How do I figure out the problem that a particular academic job is seeking to solve?

Academic jobs can seem random, and for good reason. Units rarely receive automatic replacement hires when faculty retire or leave; instead, vacated positions are almost always returned to a general pool or extinguished entirely to satisfy the budget gods. Entirely new positions may emerge in good financial times and in areas of priority growth or strong enrolment demand, while areas of weak demand or low priority may struggle regardless of the budget mood. Securing new tenure-track positions is typically a cutthroat game in which units fight each other to get positions, while simultaneously fighting within themselves about the desired area of specialization. Even securing limited-term positions can be a challenge for units, and department chairs must make compelling needs-based arguments to their deans, who may have to do the same thing at the next level.

This is the context in which academic jobs arise, and what we mean by being *a solution to their problem(s)* is that in most cases a position only emerges if someone has convinced the university that it is necessary to solve one or more problems. This problem may be rising enrolments and a need for more teaching capacity, or declining enrolments and a hope that a fresh new hire will turn that around. It could be a series of unfilled retirements (all three professors of Bushwackian studies left and were never replaced), a need to move into an emerging area of great interest (neo-Bushwackian studies now being hot), or a need to fill an embarrassing gap in expertise (it's been years since the unit has anyone who could teach and supervise in Bushwackian methods). Long story short, there is inevitably a backstory to any academic job and how the department lobbied to get it. Most of this will be opaque to you as an applicant (and rumour mills are often completely wrong), but while you likely don't know the reasons for the hiring, they are out there, and they are weighing heavily on the minds of search committee members as they read through the files.

The good news for you as an applicant is that some of the backstory may come out in the job advertisement. The job ad will ideally give you a sense of whether the department's need is primarily in the area of research (almost all tenure-track positions, even at teaching-focused universities) or teaching (most limited-term positions and specifically designated tenure-stream teaching positions). The job ad will also, to varying degrees, provide information on the ideal area of expertise: Some ads are very general and refer to a broad subfield, while others are very specific. This often depends on whether the committee prefers to make the hard decisions at the beginning or the end of the process.

The more general the ad, the more the unit has decided to defer the inevitable battle over "what we really need." Departments are also frightened by the possibility that being too specific will miss a dream candidate, even if the committee does have a pretty good idea of what they want. But don't assume that a general ad implies a simple meritocracy, based, say, on who has the strongest publishing and funding record. Everyone has their own sense of the discipline and the department's needs, and human nature means that most will consider their own particular subfield to be both (1) at the cutting edge and (2) dangerously underresourced. Committee members may think they are open minded and committed only to excellence, but blinders are always present. In contrast, specific ads typically reflect a lot of front-end work on the part of the search committee, as they identify criteria that should make the application list more manageable and the department's eventual decision easier. But since everyone is fantasizing about hypothetical dream candidates, discussions of unit needs may depart from reality as increasingly unlikely combinations

TABLE 9.1 Academic job ads explained

ADVERTISEMENT	EXPLANATION
"The Department of X invites applications for a tenure-track assistant professor position with a specialization in [broad disciplinary subfield]."	The unit is either open minded or for some reason prefers not to say what it really wants. This leaves you with limited guidance but allows you to present your strengths in whatever way best frames them.
"The Department of X seeks applications for a tenure-track appointment in [broad area]. We welcome applications from scholars specializing in Canadian, North American, South American, African, European, and/or Asian contexts, with research interests that may include, but are not limited to, apples, oranges, bananas, grapes, pears, strawberries, and pomegranates."	The unit as a whole does not know what it wants. But many individuals within it have a very good idea of what they want, and the lists reflect the competing agendas. Do your best to show how you reasonably fit as many of the criteria as possible, but without overstretching.
"The Department of X invites applications for a tenure-track appointment in [broad area]. The successful candidate will demonstrate expertise in [specific area] and/or [other specific area] with a required ability to teach [core disciplinary course]."	The unit is somewhat flexible but has a clear idea of priorities, and one of them is non-negotiable. Address as explicitly as possible how you meet all or most of their priorities in your cover letter, especially if they are not automatically evident in your CV and other materials.
"The Department of X is looking to strengthen and expand its research areas and seeks applicants with demonstrated expertise in [new and growing field]."	The unit is expanding into a new area and is not entirely sure what to expect. As with the first ad above, this gives you limited guidance but a lot of freedom. Ensure you are clearly addressing the priority area and why you have the expertise they need.
"The Department of X invites applications for a tenure-track position. The successful candidate must have the demonstrable ability to teach a first-year course in loopadoop studies, a second-year course in boobadoop studies, a third-year course in scoopadoop studies, and upper-year seminars in advanced doop theory."	While such specific requirements are common for short-term positions, they are not for a tenure-track position, and this wording suggests an inside job—the unit likely has a specific candidate in mind and the ad is tailored to their experience. See more on how to respond to this below.

("we need an expert in nineteenth-century East Asian pottery who can teach statistics and run our internship program") are envisioned and ads may get longwinded with carefully negotiated phrasings like "including but not limited to" or "ability to teach in ___ would be an asset." Read the ad closely for clues that will help you decide how to proceed.

Beyond the job ad, you can try to figure out the problem that the department is hiring to solve by doing some basic research on the department, its faculty, and the university. How does the department describe itself? Is there a strategic plan available? What programs does the department offer? Does the department seem to emphasize research or teaching? Graduate or undergraduate programs? Does the department appear to be growing or shrinking over time? Does it appear to be moving to a more research-intensive culture over time? Has it recently undergone any sort of renewal or change (such as a number of faculty retirements or recent hires)? What is the current faculty complement like? Are there clusters of interests, a broad coverage of the discipline, or a bit of both? What kinds of research publications are the faculty members producing? Do the faculty members hold numerous grants or fellowships? Overall, based on the information you can glean from the website, how do you think the department sees itself and its future? How does the department appear to tie into the goals and vision of the larger faculty and the university as a whole?

Together, the job ad and your deep-dive examination of the department and its larger institutional context will help you estimate the department's problem that it is hiring to solve. You can then use all of this information to decide if you want to apply, and if so, how to frame your application to help position yourself as the solution to their problem.

How do I decide if I fit the position enough to apply?

While one option is to apply anywhere and everywhere, doing so limits your time and ability to tailor applications to fit the particular problem the unit is trying to solve. If you are interested in a position and it is a general ad in your area, the obvious choice is to apply.

TABLE 9.2 Worksheet: Determining the departmental problem to be solved by hiring

Type of position: tenure or term
Ad emphasis: research or teaching
Mandatory fields listed in ad
Optional fields listed in ad
Undergraduate and graduate programs offered by department
Department faculty complement: - Number of faculty members - Areas of departmental research strength
How department describes itself and its goals
How faculty describes itself and its goals
How university describes itself and its goals

For more specific ads, reflect carefully on whether you can make a claim to fit the specifications that might not be immediately obvious, or how you might fit into related areas that might also appeal to the search committee. Careful reading of the job ad may help; if the ad includes definitive language like "must be able to teach advanced courses in the history of tortillas," that factor will typically be crucial. However, sometimes even the definitive factors will be flexible, either because of interpretation (candidates that only have experience in introductory tortilla history might still be considered) or if the unit is underwhelmed with its applicant pool ("We just have a couple of okay tortilla applicants, but here's an awesome taco specialist"). More conditional job ad language like "an ability to teach in the history of tortillas would be an asset" is a signal of interest but not necessarily a deal breaker, and you might be able to bolster your chances by playing up how you fit a closely related area. If you cannot position yourself in either the definitive or the conditional language, give careful thought to whether the application is a good use of your time. It is always possible that your impressive record will cause the search committee to rethink its original priorities, but don't get your hopes up.

Should you apply to positions that seem like they have an inside candidate in mind? While it may seem like a waste of your time, it is possible that (1) there isn't really an inside candidate at all (again, the rumour mill may be completely wrong), or (2) the inside candidate may choose not to apply for some reason (bad news for the hiring department, but great news for you), or (3) the search committee, forced to complete a full search by university regulations, will be more impressed by another candidate and ultimately offer the job to that person (rare, perhaps, but certainly possible). Given the relative scarcity of tenure-track academic positions, your best decision is to apply for all positions that you feel qualified for, even if there may be an inside candidate. (And if you are a potential inside candidate, see below.)

While you want to be realistic about how far you can stretch, don't necessarily rule yourself out even if you think you don't completely fit the ad or it appears that there is a preordained insider. And for all applications, it can be an advantage to mention your ability to cover perennial department teaching needs (such as foundational, theory, or research methods classes), even if they don't explicitly ask about these areas.

How I can make my application materials more competitive?

As explained in chapter 8, your goal with job applications is to secure an interview, and to do so you must present yourself as the solution to the organization's problem. Academia is not an exception to these principles, but academic applications do have some unique characteristics. One is the relative similarity of applicant profiles; while also possible in other sectors, most academic applicants present superficially uniform histories (degrees in the discipline culminating in a PhD, a nearly or recently completed dissertation, some publications, some teaching experience, etc.) making it hard for individual applications to stand out at first glance. But a second characteristic is the amount of space you are given to make your case, and thus to make yourself stand out. In other sectors, most job advertisements ask for relatively minimal materials, such as a cover letter and résumé, but academic jobs invite a truckload of material. This open-ended invitation gives you opportunities to shape your application in ways that best extol your strengths and qualities, to spin areas of potential weakness more positively, and generally to frame your record in a manner that fits the department's needs.

As we discussed cover letters, CVs, and references in chapter 8, here we focus on the elements specific to (although not always required for) academic job applications: research statements and teaching dossiers. Keep in mind that you will want to examine *all* elements of your application through the perspective of the departmental need—especially your cover letter, which is the single best opportunity to present yourself as an integrated solution to whatever that need might be. Remember that because all hiring is about addressing problems, shortlisting is only somewhat about the specific merits of your file and your achievements. Your stated areas of expertise, your dissertation topic, the places you've published, and many other things will be scrutinized for clues about whether your interests are indeed "what we really need." If the ad is more specific, it allows you to create a more tailored case that you are the answer to their particular need. If the ad is more general, it presents a greater challenge for you as an applicant, but you will still want to do whatever you can to make an explicit connection between your record and their needs. For example, application materials for a limited-term lecturer or teaching-stream tenure-track position should play up teaching, while materials for a traditional tenure-track position should highlight research.

Research statement

Your research statement has two objectives: (1) to demonstrate that you have a clear, meaningful scholarly agenda, and (2) that this agenda complements the department's own priorities. It is important to pull the threads of your previous research together into a narrative and to have concrete future plans that advance your scholarly agenda. Ideally you will be able to use your publication and grant history to provide solid evidence of your success. You need the search committee to easily understand why your research matters, who your audiences are, what theoretical traditions you are drawing from and what body of literature you are advancing, and your research methodologies. If you cannot excite the search committee about your research trajectory, your chances of making a short list are pretty low. Committees are also looking for red flags, such as a lack of scholarly publications or a lack of distinction between the candidate and the supervisor's research programs (in most disciplines). You cannot change your record, but you can use the research statement to present your strengths as forcefully as possible.

The issue of complementarity with the department is tricky and speaks to the issue of hiring being about fit as much as it is about "quality" or "merit." Approach this issue with some caution. While you might be tempted to write, "I would be able to collaborate with Dr. Bigshot," it is possible that Dr. Bigshot will be offended (why would she want to work with you? She is a rock star!), or, conversely, that everyone other than Dr. Bigshot will be offended ("Oh, great, another hanger-on for Dr. Bigshot. No thanks.") A safer course of action is to speak more broadly: "My work fits well with the department's existing research strength in the area of X, and particularly the work of Dr. Bigshot, Dr. Newcomer, and Dr. Mid-Career."

Teaching dossier

The significance of teaching will vary by the type of position and institution. Smaller, undergraduate-focused departments and more teaching-oriented positions can be expected to pay particular attention to teaching and will want to see a reasonable level of previous teaching experience, showing you're battle tested and can take on classes immediately. A place that thinks highly of its research reputation or that is striving to become more research intensive might pay less attention to your teaching experience, assuming you picked up some skills along the way. However, no one wants a complete disaster in the classroom. If your record includes no teaching whatsoever, hints of poor teaching, or suggestions that you are uninterested in teaching, these points will be raised as a red flag in your file.

If you are required to submit a teaching portfolio, statement, or philosophy, keep it short, structured, and evidence based. Supplement it with a clear list of all classes you have taught, with details about course name and level, class size, and if you were the sole instructor. You can list teaching assistant work as well; though this will usually not be given much weight itself, it at least serves as some teaching experience. If you took our earlier advice to avail yourself of different training programs available to you as a PhD student, you have likely completed some form of teaching effectiveness training, and this should be highlighted since it is evidence of your commitment to teaching. It is also helpful to review the hiring department's course offerings and draw parallels between what you are capable of teaching and the courses they have on their books. You want to be cautious not to sound like you expect to be assigned these courses (and your earnest "I would really like to teach Basketweaving 307" might step on the toes of a faculty member who feels he "owns" that particular course), but at the same time it is useful to the search committee to know where you can fit in among the existing course offerings and provide ideas of what existing courses you would be particularly suited to teach. A statement that "My background qualifies me to teach a number of courses in the department's existing catalogue, including (list of course numbers and names)" will do the trick; if that list includes perennial core courses, all the better.

What do I need to consider if I am an "inside candidate"?

One of the toughest aspects of academic hiring is when some candidates are already on the premises or otherwise well known. From the outside, it might seem they have an obvious inside track. This can be true for limited-term positions where the unit has to fill an immediate need and prefers to play it safe, but the opposite situation can occur with tenure-track hires. Units are prone to thinking the grass is greener on the other side, so they may spurn known people in search of "the very best." While some searches do seem to resemble a romantic comedy—a department searches around the world for someone to be its true love, only to discover the person was right there all along in the office next door—inside candidates for tenure-track positions can face particular challenges.

It is helpful to break this down into two different types of insiders.

- *The department's own PhDs:* Academic departments may be reluctant to hire their own PhD graduates for tenure-track positions.

A PhD's view of the discipline will have been profoundly shaped by their doctoral experience (if it didn't, they wasted five or more years in grad school), and that experience, for better or worse, replicated the norms, cultures, and views of their doctoral department. Hiring the department's own PhDs risks perpetuating the same norms and assumptions; given that change happens slowly in academic units, outside hirings are the best way an academic unit can refresh itself and bring in new perspectives and ideas. This may seem unfair ("If they've given me a PhD and recommended me for other jobs, surely I'm good enough for them, too"), but the logic is strong for tenure-track positions. It weakens if the applicant has gone somewhere else in between; having a postdoc, term, or ideally a tenure-track position at another institution can potentially reset everything, because it shows the applicant was indeed good enough to be taken on elsewhere and hopefully learned some new things beyond their PhD. And the argument can reverse for limited-term positions, which are primarily about short-term teaching needs, so an insider who can hit the ground running may be an asset.

- *The department's sessional instructors, lecturers, and postdocs:* A different challenge confronts candidates who earned their PhD elsewhere but are now in the hiring department as sessional lecturers, postdocs, or other short-term affiliations and are literally just down the hall. As noted above, for limited-term positions, local candidates may have a clear "hit the ground running" advantage. But tenure-track positions are more complicated. Inside candidates are familiar and make search committees feel comfortable—but perhaps too comfortable, and the committee pines for the glamour and mystery of new people. Some inside candidates have had their research productivity sidelined by teaching, rendering their CVs less competitive, regardless of how much the committee members like them at a personal level. There's no easy answer here.

Regardless of whether you are an internal or external candidate, start from the assumption that the unit is trying to run the fairest competition it can. And if you are a potential inside candidate, see Table 9.3.

TABLE 9.3 What to do if you are an inside candidate

	... AND THE JOB IS A TERM POSITION	... AND THE JOB IS A TENURE-TRACK POSITION
You received your PhD from the hiring department ..	You are in a strong position if you clearly fit the general area they are looking for, have some course instructor experience, have a completed dissertation or defence date, and have a general reputation around the unit for professionalism, agreeableness, and non-prima-donna behaviour. **Your mission**: Make sure taking such a position is in your best interest. Devise a plan to balance the teaching loads associated with term positions so that you do not end up sidelining activities (including publishing) that advance your larger career objectives. (See our chapter 8 discussion of the sessional trap.)	Accept the inbreeding argument, but do everything possible to show it doesn't apply to you. **Your mission**: Apart from a great dissertation and high-quality publications (applicable everywhere), seek to demonstrate *external* scholarly validity: disciplinary awards, grants, research projects, and partnerships with people at other universities, extra training at other institutions (e.g., summer schools), links to Great Eminences with no ties to your home unit, and so on. The odds are still against you, but give the committee as much hard evidence as possible to demonstrate you are more than just a familiar face.
You are a sessional/ postdoc in the hiring department, but your PhD is from somewhere else ..	See above.	You have a decent shot, provided your research record is competitive and you fit the job description. Solid publishing and funding records are incalculably important. **Your mission**: Do everything possible to avoid complications. Seek a frank conversation with the department chair and others to demonstrate you understand the complexities and seek their procedural advice. (This wins you additional points for good citizenship.) Make it clear that you realize you are not a sure thing, but do it so graciously that people begin thinking about what a sure thing you would be.

What do I do after I have applied for a job?

Having sweated every detail of their application, job applicants wait ... and wait. Why can't they at least tell me I didn't make it? Why haven't I heard a thing? These are reasonable questions, but here's some reasons why departments don't get back to you quickly.

First, the process isn't as clear as you might think. Short lists may come together gradually and conditionally and often need to be approved by deans, human resources offices, or others. Departments also do not want to shut doors prematurely: You might not be on the first interview short list, but a candidate may drop out and you may get a late call, or the search committee may fail to agree on any of the first interviewed candidates and choose to conduct a second round of interviews. Things drag out and there's rarely a single clear moment when your application officially doesn't make it. Second, sending out notices to a large number of unsuccessful applicants can be administratively complex; hirings are not part of the regular office routine and staff support is often limited. And third, they're afraid you will sue them. Human resources and legal advisors inevitably recommend caution and minimal or no communication at every turn to avoid complications, and they usually advise units not to contact applicants before the position is finally filled. Bottom line: Other than possibly emailing the department assistant—not the chair, not a faculty member—to confirm receipt of your application or to inform the search committee of a *substantial* change to your application (e.g., your PhD was successfully defended or you won an important grant or award since the time you submitted your application), do not contact the department about your application.

Our experience: Jonathan

Short lists do change, and that's how I got on the list for my position. There were three candidates reflecting three different specialties. One dropped off, and I was the backup for that specialty, so they called me. I didn't know that at the time, and I'm not sure I would have wanted to know it at the time of the interview.

I received an invitation for an interview. How do I prepare?

While in the United States it is standard in most disciplines to start with a long list and conduct initial interviews at major conferences or by telephone before moving to a short list of campus interviews, in Canada it is not uncommon to go straight to a short list with one- or two-day campus interviews. These typically consist of a "job talk," a formal committee interview, get-to-know-you meals, meetings with students, an undergraduate lecture, and meetings with the department chair and the dean.

Campus interviews focus on the candidate's ability to grow and flourish as a scholar. Search committees usually have a good sense of each candidate's strengths from the file, but while it is rare that a candidate unexpectedly blows everyone away, occasionally candidates turn out to be less impressive than the committee expected. Because of this, preparing for all aspects of the campus interview and showing you have a strong forward trajectory is critical. You need to prepare on at least three fronts: *job talk*, *interview*, and *background research* on the department and its faculty members. If you are asked to do a *teaching demonstration*, you need to prepare this as well. Be sure to inquire about basic expectations, including how long your presentations should be, to inform your preparations.

Sample interview itinerary

Evening before – Candidate arrives, takes taxi to hotel

8:00 a.m. – Faculty member picks up candidate at hotel

8:30 a.m. – Candidate meets with department chair

9:15 a.m. – Candidate meets with faculty ("meet and greet")

9:30 a.m. – Research presentation (aka "job talk")

11:00 a.m. – Candidate break in private office

11:15 a.m. – Candidate meets with dean

12:00 p.m. – Lunch with five faculty members

1:15 p.m. – Interview with search committee

2:45 p.m. – Candidate meets with students

3:30 p.m. – Candidate delivers 30-minute lecture in ongoing undergraduate class

4:30 p.m. – Campus tour with student association representatives

5:00 p.m. – City tour with two faculty members

6:30 p.m. – Dinner with four faculty members

Next morning – Candidate takes taxi to airport

Job talk

For the job talk, ask for clarity on its exact format. How long would they like you to speak, and how much time will be available for questions? Do they want you to present specific research, an overview of your research program, or some combination of the two? Who will be in the audience? Will there be presentation equipment? Make no assumptions whatsoever; while many units favour a 30–40 minute public talk followed by questions, there are numerous formats. Once you know what is requested of you, make strategic decisions regarding how narrow versus comprehensive, and general versus specific, you should be. Estimate, based on what you have learned about the audience, how familiar they will already be with the literature, key debates, and methodology. You need to be completely confident and in control of what you're talking about, so this is not the time to present early results, experiment with new ideas, muse about future plans, or generally present anything less than a finished (or nearly finished) project. Be careful with your use of presentation software; your slides should be visually appealing, professional, and simply a value-added to your presentation, rather than the focal point.

Job talk checklist

- ❏ Clearly stated research question
- ❏ Clearly stated link to theoretical framework(s)
- ❏ Clear explanation of methodology
- ❏ Clearly stated answer to research question
- ❏ Clear explanation of why your work is an important contribution to scholarship in your discipline
- ❏ Clear explanation of how the research you are presenting links to your larger scholarly trajectory
- ❏ Clear link between your research and the advertised position (have we mentioned that "fit" is critical?)
- ❏ Prepared, clear answers to obvious and less than obvious questions regarding your research
- ❏ Energy and enthusiasm (if you don't seem to care about your topic, no one else will)

We used the word "clear" repeatedly in this checklist, not because we are in need of a thesaurus but rather to encourage you to be deliberate about what you are trying to accomplish in the job talk and to be explicit in providing the search committee with the information it needs for you to accomplish these objectives.

Once you have prepared your job talk, practise. For the love of all that is blessed and holy, practise the job talk. Be prepared in case technology fails you. A candidate who manages to give a riveting presentation despite being unexpectedly deprived of her slides will be vividly remembered. Even a fair performance despite unexpected disruption will be respected. Rehearse the talk with an audience (ideally a group that simulates your anticipated audience as much as possible, both in size and familiarity with your field)—if your graduate program doesn't already provide opportunities to practise job talks, ask them to start. Time it carefully to be absolutely sure you can finish in the time you were given. Listen carefully to feedback about the clarity and coherence of the talk, and of course for questions you hadn't anticipated … including and especially ones you find elementary or even stupid. Avoid politely worded responses that essentially convey "you don't understand this methodology" and "I'm sorry that you can't grasp my argument." Practise taking every question seriously; even if a question seems profoundly misguided, answer it respectfully. It can be difficult to know when to push back and stand by your argument without seeming defensive, but practice can help you discern when to stand firm. Most of all, anticipate the "so what?" question: Why should other scholars care, and how does this fit and engage with current literature and debates? Great job talks are rare; your goal is simply a good, solid one that backs up the promise of your written file.

Our experience: Loleen

My job talk for my current position did not go as I anticipated. The talk began a half hour later than I expected, I had prepared a 45-minute talk and was startled to be passed a "5 minutes left" note from the chair at the 30-minute mark, and the question and answer session covered topics well beyond my presentation. It was stressful, but ultimately everything worked out.

Formal interview

Positions are often won at the formal interview. Again, ask the department for clarity on length of time and who will be present. Cover all of the interview preparation steps that we identified in chapter 8, with careful attention to identifying concrete narrative examples as opposed to general platitudes. And, as we recommended in chapter 8, practise your responses to predictable questions (see the list below) extensively. The search committee wants to gather as much information as possible about your current and prospective research and your larger ambitions so that it can picture the trajectory of your future career. As you practice, watch for answers that could be seen as critical or negative; for example, your argument that lecturing is a terrible teaching approach may not be welcomed by the faculty members who prefer a lecture format. Resist the temptation to denigrate any scholar or body of work; you don't know these people well enough for such candour.

Background research

It is in your interest to have a full understanding of the department and its faculty before you arrive. Build upon your previous background research on the department, faculty, and university to gain an understanding of individual people, and review all of this information carefully. (You can assume that the other candidates took the time to do so, and if they didn't, that's good news for you.) Any question you ask that could be reasonably answered by looking at the department or university website may be held against you, whereas questions for further details on something you saw on the website ("I noticed you offer a certificate program in Antarctic Urban Planning; can you tell me more about that?") will be held in your favour. A thorough study of the department's website combined with searches on key individuals—those working in your subfield, at the very least—will not only help you anticipate potential questions they might ask at the job talk and interview, but also help prepare you for the social elements. Keep in mind that in addition to believing your research adds value to the discipline and your teaching will add value to their program, the search committee needs to be reasonably convinced that they want to work with you for the next 20 or 30 years. Simply put, you need to be likeable. While it is vital to guard against insincere flattery ("I think your book is the greatest publication ever"), your

TABLE 9.4 Worksheet: Academic interview questions you must be prepared for

QUESTION	TIPS	YOUR RESPONSE
How does your research plan go beyond your dissertation work? What is your five-year research plan, including publication plans (with journals/book publishers specified), research grant plans (with funding agencies specified), and timelines?	You will almost certainly be asked these questions and you should have good but realistic answers. The more specific you can be, the better.	
How is your work independent from that of your supervisor?	This may vary by discipline but is likely to come up if there are close connections (especially co-publications) with your supervisor. More than a few candidates have failed to convince committees they can move beyond their supervisor's orbit.	
If you could design and teach any course, what would it be?	This chestnut tells a committee a lot about what makes you tick, and they'll probe what you would put in or leave out.	
How do you manage diversity in the classroom? Give us an example of how you have implemented your teaching philosophy in the classroom. How do you balance research and teaching?	As noted in chapter 8, aim to share actual narrative experiences and concrete examples.	
All questions listed in chapter 8 (and particularly "What interests you about this position?" "What would make you a good colleague?" and "Do you have any questions for us?")	Many interview questions are ubiquitous regardless of the sector. Anticipate these, and prepare responses that draw on narrative experiences to make a compelling case for yourself. And again, have a prepared written list of questions for them that demonstrates you have done your homework on the unit and are serious about the position.	

TABLE 9.5 Worksheet: Faculty background research

FACULTY MEMBER	RESEARCH AND TEACHING AREAS	NOTES (GRANTS, AWARDS, CROSS-APPOINTMENTS, BACKGROUND, NOTABLE PUBLICATIONS, MAJOR SERVICE POSITIONS SUCH AS GRADUATE OR UNDERGRADUATE CHAIR, ETC.)
Chair		
Professor A		
Assistant Professor B		
Associate Professor C		
...		
Assistant Professor Z		

background research demonstrates that you are exceptionally well prepared and have done your homework, and people will remember and appreciate that.

Remember that you are always "on" and always being assessed, from the moment you are picked up at the airport (if the department does this) to the casual walks between scheduled activities until the very last goodbye. Prepare for stressful situations and deal with them in advance when possible (assume that the airline will lose your luggage and that technology will fail). Meals are unlikely to make or break a candidate by themselves, but they reinforce overall impressions. They are also the most likely time when conversations will veer into personal (possibly legally prohibited) questions, such as whether you have a partner or children. This is a difficult conundrum, as mentioning personal circumstances might be benign or even to your advantage, or it may subtly or overtly change attitudes to your disadvantage. Trust your instincts and your own comfort level, and remember that you are not required to say anything here.

Teaching demonstration
Being dropped into a pre-existing class to deliver a lecture to undergraduates whose main concern is, "Will this be on the exam?" is

challenging, to say the least. Your goal here is to demonstrate a sense of your teaching style and convey your professionalism and authority in the classroom. Ask to contact the course instructor and for a copy of the syllabus to familiarize yourself with the readings or textbook. Determine exactly how long your teaching demonstration should take and the availability of technology.

Ensure your demonstration is authentic to who you are as a teacher. Build in notes for yourself about the expected timing, and have backup plans if the material runs short or long. If you want to demonstrate that your teaching involves student engagement, be sure to structure the activities to ensure at least some participation. (Direct questions to the class can be risky, as students stare blankly at the stranger—you—in front of them.) Again, assume that technology will fail and have a backup plan on that front. And the use of humour is great, but again exercise caution; you don't know this particular audience, and a failed joke in front of 50 students and the search committee can leave you feeling awkward. Above all, aim to show the search committee and the students that teaching matters to you, and that you will be an asset to the department on that front.

As noted in chapter 8, after the interview take the time to demonstrate gratitude for the interview opportunity through an email to the department chair and search committee members, and for the logistical support through an email to whoever helped you. And then you just wait.

Red flags to avoid raising

Failure to show interest in faculty members: People want to work with people whose company they enjoy. Showing interest—genuine interest—in getting to know the faculty in the department you are hoping to work at for the next few decades is a wise choice. Ask them what they like to teach. Ask them about their research interests. Ask them what they like about the city and where they came from originally. And ask these questions for the sake of establishing a connection, rather than as an opportunity for you to springboard to your own responses and talk about yourself. In short, be a decent, genuine human being that people will actually want to work with.

BOX 9.1: THE CAMPUS VISIT: ADD UP YOUR POINTS

Arrival

- You complain about the taxi driver or the airline (−8)
- You are curt and abrupt with the office staff (−15)
- You show up early (+5)

Job talk

- Technology doesn't work but that's okay—you brought hard copies of your tables and graphs and deliver a smooth presentation anyway (+25)
- End exactly on the time you were given (+7)
- Go more than 5 minutes over the time you were given (−10)
- End well before the time you were given (−15)
- Roll your eyes or get defensive at a question (−15)
- Give a gracious answer to the question from "Ol' Grumpy" (+10)

Interview

- When asked what new courses you'd like to develop, produce the sample outline you've already written (+7)
- Criticize your doctoral/current department (−25)
- Lay out your publication plans for each chapter of your dissertation (+12)
- When asked about new research plans: "I'm not really sure yet; do you guys have any suggestions?" (−50)
- At the end when the committee asks, "Do you have any questions for us?"
    - ask a question about university support for grant applications (+8)
    - ask about parking (−8)

Dinner

- "No thank you, one glass of wine is fine." (+4)
- "Wow, look at this list of craft brews! I'm going to try a bunch!" (−15)

- Use the wrong fork (0)
- Tell someone else they're using the wrong fork (−20)

Miscellaneous

- Meeting with students:
  - Give a conspiratorial wink and ask, "C'mon, tell me what this place is really like." (−12)
  - Ask what their experience has been like in the program (+9)
- Say you are only interested in the position until something at a better university opens up (−100)

Scoring

There is no formula, but higher is always better.

Appearing superior: We get it: You are nervous, want the job, and want to impress. And this desire can lead you to want to mention—again, and oh, perhaps, yet again—your work at Prestigious University, your cutting-edge methodological training, your coauthored article with Dr. Smartypants in the *International Journal of Super-High Impact Factor.* This desire can lead you to want to mention your ideas for how the department can modernize its outdated curriculum, do a better job at engaging students, and use more innovative teaching practices. This desire to impress can lead you to want to hint that your research potential means you will be able to double the amount of research money coming into the department. It might even tempt you to reassure the faculty that while you come from the Big City with all of its wonderful amenities, you are willing to deign to work at Hinterlands University, despite its six-month winter and lack of a doctoral program. Curb these desires.

Negativity: Negative people wear people down, including themselves. The flight was okay, except for the crying baby and the layover. The hotel wasn't *that* terrible. Teaching is great, except the grading and having to deal with unprepared students. Departments are typically already equipped with a resident doom-and-gloom Eeyore or a resident curmudgeon (some even have multiples of each!), so go in the opposite direction. You don't have to fake perky upbeatness, but pretty much every complaint of any kind during the interview visit, no matter how unrelated to academia, is a nail in your coffin.

I haven't heard back after my interview. Why is it taking so long?

Search processes are often long, which can be agonizing for the candidates. After departments complete their interviews (which can be spread over a fair period of time, depending on the number of candidates being interviewed), the search committee must come to a decision about which candidate, if any, to offer the position to. There are usually multiple levels of approval at the university and everyone may need to sign off before anything happens at all. Often, the department chair will informally contact the recommended candidate to let them know the recommendation was made, but this may be prohibited by institutional rules. It is also possible that you have not heard a thing because you are ranked second or third and will not receive an offer unless the first-ranked candidate chooses to turn the offer down. This might be a bit ego-bruising to consider, but your goal is to land the job, and patience may be required.

What are the chances of a position for my spouse/partner?

Since taking an academic job typically means moving to a new city, the "two-body problem" is well established for couples both looking for academic jobs. While it is possible that a job offer can be used to negotiate a position for your partner, this requires a tricky mix of delicate and hard-nosed negotiation, with most factors outside your control. Success typically depends on two things: the university's budgetary situation at the moment and how badly they want you. While the chances are admittedly low, this issue is so common in academia that it is always worth asking.

Overall, how should I approach the academic job market?

We started this chapter noting that academic job markets can seem like lotteries, with improbable odds and a reliance on pure luck. While our suggestions can help you position yourself as the best fit for a particular academic position, there is still a significant dimension of luck in play. Some PhDs are fortunate to have the opportunity to apply for positions that directly match their areas of expertise, making it easier for them to make the case that they are in fact the solution to a department's problem, but for others, the seemingly easy fit does not suddenly appear. And even for those who have the fortune of being able to apply to positions that match their expertise, there is still the challenging reality that there may be others who can also make a strong case and the unit can only choose one of you.

Throughout this book we have encouraged you to focus on the larger goal of a successful, rewarding career that uses your talents and the skills that you developed throughout your education. Academia is one such career, and if the right opportunity opens up for you we wish you all the success; universities need smart, industrious new faculty as they evolve to continue to meet society's needs. At the same time, there are so many opportunities for you, and so many ways you can use your doctoral education in a rewarding manner. You have competencies, training, and knowledge that will be the solution to someone's hiring problem.

So, how should you approach the academic job market? You should pursue academic jobs at the same time as pursuing jobs in other sectors. You should continue to go on informational interviews, build your networks, expand your skills, and create evidence of your amazing career competencies. You should continue to publish and remain active in your scholarly community. And, wherever you end up, you should continue to assess opportunities and actions in light of your future goals and the information available to you.

CHAPTER 10

WORK YOUR CAREER

In the preceding pages, we have occasionally explained our ideas by referencing dated (although we prefer the word "timeless") pop culture. We shall indulge this format a final time by drawing upon the iconic 1986 film *Ferris Bueller's Day Off*, specifically to invoke the immortal words of the titular character, who states, "Life moves pretty fast. If you don't stop and look around once in a while, you could miss it."

Your PhD program, your career, your life as a whole are yours and yours alone. As we said in chapter 1, one size does not fit all, and we have worked to reinforce this fact throughout this book. Not only is there is no single "right" or "best" path, it's vital to stop and look around to make sure you aren't missing what's best for your life. Throughout these chapters, we have returned to two key ideas. The first is to encourage you to embrace your personal agency, to actively *work your career* from the start, rather than passively moving through your program, because life does move pretty fast. The second is to encourage you to be thoughtful and strategic in your choices, looking around continually—not just every once in a while—and asking yourself, Given both my future goals and the information currently available to me, what is my best decision right now? To achieve your goals, we suggested that you invest your time and energy wisely. That you focus on competency and network development in addition to content mastery. That you take steps to become the professional you aspire to be. That you assess what the possibilities are for your current situation, rather than assuming you have somehow run out of time. And that, throughout it all, you pay close attention to the tone you are setting, for yourself and for those around you.

Our experience: Jonathan

When I was finishing my PhD, I was very pessimistic about my job prospects. My partner and I had set definite geographic boundaries on what positions to consider, and while I was already heavily embarked on pursuing a variety of career options, I was encountering only closed doors and terse rejections. But I remember one day, as I was listening to the radio while revising my dissertation yet again, when one of my favourite songs came on. I can still picture that moment, because I suddenly felt really good, and I remember the feeling—with no job yet in sight and the plan going awry—that not only had I done good stuff in grad school that no one could ever take away, but that life was good and something would turn up for me. I knew the best was yet to come. I still believe that, and I believe it for others as well. The best is yet to come.

And now you are here. You are done reading this book, and possibly approaching the end of your PhD program, be it through finishing the program or, equally acceptable, by choosing to take a different direction. Again, as we said in chapter 1, where you end up may not necessarily result in the outcome you expected. But by taking hold of your personal agency, by continually reassessing your choices based on your goals and the information available to you, you can be confident in your ability to make good decisions for yourself and to strategically pursue your own best interests. Your capacity to do meaningful things in your future is ultimately limited only by your imagination. It is exciting, for you and the world around you alike.

Our experience: Loleen

My career path has not been what I expected, to say the least. I am extremely grateful for this. My early-twenties self who decided to pursue a doctorate because it seemed like the obvious and easy next step lacked the imagination and wisdom to see the myriad opportunities that life would present. I still don't know what lies ahead for me, and I refuse to assume that just because I have returned to academia for now that I will remain a professor until I retire. My future goals continue to evolve, the information available to me continues to evolve, and I continue to work to make the best decisions for myself and my family. It is a process that does not end. To me, the possibilities are thrilling.

Life requires us to occasionally pause, reflect, and enjoy, and we encourage you to celebrate as well as you move forward in your career and your life. And we urge you to open up new conversations about the many opportunities for social science and humanities PhDs. We believe passionately in the potential of PhD students to contribute to our country's future, and care deeply about the well-being of individual students—so much so that it motivated us to write this book. We are, of course, not alone; there are many, many other faculty and others who care as much as we do and who will be happy to personally assist and guide you as you move forward. We encourage you to find these individuals and to open these conversations. We expect that you will be pleasantly surprised by the amount of support and mentorship available. The potential is there. Unlock it.

At the end of *Ferris Bueller's Day Off*, after the credits have run, Ferris turns to the audience and says, "You're still here? It's over. Go home. Go." We too will now draw things to a close. Go. Work your career.

FACULTY CALL TO ACTION

Work Your Career is primarily focused on an audience of potential, current, and recent PhDs and how they can exert agency to reach their personal goals. But this final message is directed at faculty and academic administrators, particularly in PhD-granting units but also across universities and disciplines as a whole, because they have agency to make broader impacts and changes to PhD career mentoring and development. We believe that faculty members and academic administrators are committed to doctoral education and care about the career futures of their students, but also that many are unclear or unsure how they can truly help students work their careers. As we've stated, there is no Supervisor School, so most faculty replicate whatever mentoring experience they had ... or did not have. Faculty by definition ended up in academia, often with limited or no work experience in other sectors, and many feel ill-equipped to guide students toward any other path. And thus prevailing academic cultures continue, with students feeling they must follow a single narrow path and privilege academic careers as the sole worthy destination, despite job market realities, the vast and rich array of other options, and the fact that Canada can benefit from the talents of PhDs in all areas of its economy and society.

After devoting the past chapters to providing advice to students, we respectfully offer the following suggestions to our colleagues in the academy. You are in a tremendous position of influence in your students' lives, and your capacity to assist them is greater than you may realize. As faculty, we set the tone for students, and for each other. We have encouraged our student readers to identify and embrace their own sphere of agency, and here we ask you to do the same. Collectively and individually, we can do better. And ethically, we must. Here is our call to action.

Provide open information and promote discussion

1. Provide clear statistical information on program completion rates and times on the departmental website. Your graduate faculty undoubtedly collects these data, and prospective, current, and former students would benefit by seeing these data without having to ask. Do not assume students "just know" how long a PhD truly takes, or the statistical likelihood that they will leave the program. Most have no idea until they are well into it.

2. Promote concrete and wide-ranging discussions about PhD career outcomes and opportunities. Celebrate the career successes—both academic and non-academic—of your PhD students, including doctoral students who left the program prior to completion. Highlight and celebrate them in department communications and through panels and events that encourage networking with current students.

3. Be an ally, not an obstacle, to students trying to work their careers. Challenge casual and not-so-casual comments that reinforce the notion that academic careers are superior to other career outcomes. Change the language away from "Plan B" and make sure that students know this is your attitude. Be there for them.

Improve programs

4. Initiate discussions within your department about whether program requirements, such as the comprehensive exam and dissertation formats, can be revised to be more career relevant,

and whether reading lists and requirements can be revised to include or expand on career-planning materials.

5. Explicitly build competency development into the PhD classes you teach. Clarify what these competencies are and how they are career relevant, and assess students on their competencies in addition to their mastery of content. For example, include an assignment in which students demonstrate their ability to write about a scholarly matter or concept for a general audience.

6. Familiarize yourself with your graduate faculty's programs and services for career training. Bring these opportunities to the attention of students and explore how they can be linked and incorporated into your programs. Encourage your department to provide students with incentives to participate, including giving students course credit.

Initiate a cultural shift

7. In your unit, discipline, and other scholarly circles, promote wider discussion of PhD career outcomes through conference panels, journal issues, research studies, and more. Encourage practical steps and solutions appropriate to your discipline and field, and keep at this. Build momentum rather than cyclical revisits of "what can we do?"

8. Blur the boundaries between academia and "other." This does not mean diluting scholarly standards and norms, but allowing and embracing a mixed approach that allows people to engage and pursue excellence in more than one context. This can be through conferences and publications, through hiring and tenure and promotion standards, and other initiatives that attract and reward people who value their doctoral education and want to continue contributing to the scholarly enterprise, but are also drawn to other paths of success.

9. Finally, work your own career. Throughout this book, we have told readers it is never too late to embrace new things, pick up new habits, discard old ones, and set new or clearer goals

that are right for them. This applies to you (and to us), and we hope many of the ideas in this book have inspired and engaged you as well. Your actions set an example to students and others who are watching and who you are consciously or unconsciously mentoring already. It's never too late to work your career.

INDEX

Lightning Source UK Ltd.
Milton Keynes UK
UKHW02f2212130618
323925UK00021B/488/P